The Complete Guide to Property Investment

How to survive and thrive in the new world of buy-to-let

Rob Dix

AN IMPORTANT NOTE FOR 2021

If you're ever tempted to write a book about an ever-changing field that's subject to 178 separate pieces of legislation – and commit to putting out a new edition annually – allow me to caution you gently against it.

Every year when I come to update this book, I'm shocked by how much has changed. And with 2020 being a bit of a funny one (to put it mildly), there's more uncertainty than usual as I sit writing this in December 2020. Eviction laws in particular have been changing from week to week (literally) lately, and there's plenty of other change afoot too.

So, rather than just printing a photo of myself shrugging at several points in the book, I've opted to include the most recent "stable" version of current laws and ignore temporary Covid-related exemptions, extensions, exceptions, etc.

To keep up with all the latest changes and other important property and economic news, I recommend you do these three things:

1. Register your purchase of this book at **propertygeek.net/extra**. This will give you access to some extra materials, and you'll start receiving my Sunday newsletter – where I share the top

property news stories of the week, with a bit of commentary about what they mean for you.

2. Subscribe to The Property Podcast, where there's a new episode every Thursday morning: **propertyhub.net/podcast**

3. Check out the wealth of educational material (which we're constantly adding to) at Property Hub (**propertyhub.net**). There you'll find videos and free courses, plus our Property Hub forum – where you can join in the discussion with thousands of other investors.

CONTENTS

THE COMPLETE GUIDE TO PROPERTY INVESTMENT

Published by Team Incredible Publishing

INTRODUCTION

Getting a UK-centric audience excited about property investment is about as challenging as getting YouTube views with a cute cat video. There are over a million private landlords in the UK, and millions more who've thought about it. A quick glance at any day's newspaper headlines, meanwhile, will show that everyone else has a very strong opinion about it.

Technically, all that's needed to call yourself a "property investor" is to buy one house or flat and rent it out – and if you do that well, you'll have an asset that will bring in money each month and grow in value over time. That's pretty good, and it will put you ahead of the 80% of the population who just work all their lives and retire without any real assets to show for it.

But the game is changing. As political pressure against landlords mounts and the tax regime changes, it's becoming impossible to be a casual buy-any-old-house-and-watch-it-go-up-in-value investor. Strange as it may seem though, I think the coming years will be better than ever – for educated and committed investors, at least. Amateurs will get squeezed out of the market, leaving opportunities wide open for those of us who are switched-on, strategic, and in it for the long haul.

Even if changes *weren't* afoot, I still think we can – indeed should – aim higher than just buying the odd property when we can. After all, for most of us the ultimate dream isn't an extra couple of hundred pounds in our pocket each month or bragging rights at dinner parties. There's some kind of goal we're aiming for, like securing a comfortable retirement or being able to support our family without leaving for the office at 7am every day. Property can be the means to that end... but unless we're clear on what the objective actually *is*, it can easily just be a source of hassle and disappointment.

Over the last few years I've spoken to hundreds of aspiring and established investors. Often, they'll ask for my advice because they're not sure where to start – or they'll be disappointed because they've got going and bought a property, but still don't feel much closer to where they want to be. In almost every case, the problem would be solved if they just had a meaningful goal paired with a clear strategy designed to help them reach it.

But I'm rarely asked about that – instead the questions are about what mortgage to use, how much to pay for a specific property, whether or not to self-manage, what research to do before buying at auction, and a million other things about the "procedural" aspect of property investment. These are all perfectly good and valid questions... but they're all secondary concerns until a goal has been set and a strategy sketched out.

In this book, I'm going to cover it all: the strategic overview, the nitty-gritty procedural details, and everything you need to know to adapt and thrive over time – whatever the economy and the politicians throw your way.

By calling this the "complete guide", I know I'm leaving myself wide open for people to go through looking for flaws, errors and omissions. If you go in search of things to disagree with, you'll find plenty: as this is a book written by one person, there will be some parts that you don't think are explained fully enough and others where you don't agree with my reasoning.

When it comes to the word "complete" itself, I don't mean that it will cover every situation that you could possibly encounter over a lifetime of investing in property – clearly, that's not possible. What I mean is that it takes you through the entire process of becoming a successful investor. **Most books focus on how to research and buy a single property, but this one starts way before the first purchase and doesn't stop until you've built a long-term portfolio.**

In Part 1, I get you thinking about your goals by showing you five different investment strategies that you *could* follow – each suitable for different objectives, financial positions and levels of involvement. The aim is to give you a vision of what you can achieve – even if you're starting out with no special skills or experience.

In Part 2, we'll go through every step of the property investment process in order. Starting with arranging finance, we'll advance through deciding what to buy, assessing potential deals, getting an offer accepted, surviving the buying process, and going all the way through to managing the property and taking care of the paperwork. You can read it through to prepare yourself for exactly what's ahead, then refer back to each chapter as you progress through an actual investment to make sure you're confident at every step.

Then in Part 3, it's time to look at the topics that separate the "dabblers" who buy a property on a whim from those who are serious about building a long-term financial future: refinancing, surviving downturns, shaping your portfolio over time and thinking about an eventual exit strategy.

Overall, everything in this book is geared towards helping you to take action. It's not telling you "how I did it" and giving you one model to follow, it's not an inspirational story, and it's not a boring list of first-do-this-then-do-that. It's designed to take you from wherever you are now to wherever you want to be, by arming you with both the procedural knowledge and the big-picture thinking you need to make smart decisions.

If property isn't your obsession yet, I hope it will be by the end of this book: not only is it one of the most profitable things you can be obsessed with, it's also a whole lot of fun.

ABOUT ME

While this book is intended to serve you rather than my ego, it might be helpful to give you a bit of context so you know who I am and where I'm coming from.

Property investment is the geeky hobby that took over my life.

As soon as I started researching my first investment in 2006 as a place to stash some spare cash, I was hooked. I'd spend all my spare time reading books and message boards – and yes, watching a fair bit of Homes Under The Hammer – absorbing everything I possibly could.

I was fascinated by the number of ways in which it was possible to approach property investment, and I began to see how success involves understanding human psychology (and understanding your own abilities and motivations) in addition to knowing the cold, hard numbers.

As a happy side-effect, I loved the fact that – as hobbies go – it can make you seriously wealthy.

In 2012 I started my blog, Property Geek, as a place to think out loud and make contact with other investors so I could learn even more. Since then, property has almost completely taken over...

- I've written four best-selling property books, which have well over 1,000 five-star reviews on Amazon between them.

- I co-present The Property Podcast, which is the most popular business podcast in the UK and is listened to more than 300,000 times per month.

- I co-founded Property Hub (**propertyhub.net**) – a community for property investors with over 40,000 members, which offers various services to investors and also publishes a bi-monthly magazine.

I don't have the UK's biggest portfolio or decades of experience, but I've supplemented my own knowledge and experience with learning from hundreds of investors who I've had the pleasure to meet and quiz. It means that if I haven't done it myself, I've spoken (at length) to multiple people who have.

My own strategy? Well, it's evolved over time – and I've certainly had my fair share of getting sidetracked. When I started out, all I cared about was buying as much rental income as I could, as cheaply as possible. That approach led me to good-quality ex-council flats in London, which nobody else wanted to buy – especially after the mid-2000s crash – yet rented spectacularly well to young professionals. Over time I came to think more in terms of *total asset growth*: parking my savings in quality properties that make me money each month but also have good growth potential. Additionally, I began adding to those savings by flipping the odd property where possible. (I can't shake my old yield-monkey tendencies completely though, and occasionally I'll buy properties with limited growth potential if I can get a great return while leaving little cash in the deal.)

The ultimate plan? To be in a "work optional" situation, with a big lump sum in the bank and a few moderately leveraged properties generating a nice income, at a young enough age to mean I can pursue whatever seems interesting at the time without money being a factor.

Just to be clear: I'm not a tycoon with hundreds of properties, and there are many, *many*, **many** investors who are vastly more successful than I am. If there's one specific strategy or aspect of investment you want to know about, there will be someone more qualified than me to teach you about it. But what I *can* do is give you an easy-to-understand, comprehensive and hopefully fun overview of the whole property landscape.

So let's get on and do exactly that.

PART 1:
STRATEGIES

Introduction

In this first part of the book, I'm going to explore five potential investment strategies – each of which requires a different amount of cash and time input, and pays off over a different timeframe.

If you're just starting out, feel free to flip through them to get a general sense of what the options are – but don't go any further with planning out your next moves until you've clearly defined your *goal*.

You might think you've got a goal already, but if you were forced to get it out of your head and onto paper it'd probably look embarrassingly vague. A goal like "own lots of properties" or "eventually reach the point of not having to work for someone else" just isn't going to cut it – you need more precision in order to select the strategy that's best suited to getting you there.

When it comes to setting a goal, there are three elements that I think are the most important:

1. It needs to be specific enough that you'll know when you've achieved it – which is where "lots of properties"

try to be careful enough with my numbers elsewhere that it doesn't matter too much.

Then there's tax. I mention the possible impact of tax in each scenario, but it's impossible to make statements like "your tax bill from this transaction will be £X" or "make sure you set aside £Y". The answer will be different depending on your other sources of earnings, marital status, whether the property is owned by an individual or a company, other property transactions you've made that year, and about a million other things.

So the results I talk about are *always pre-tax* – not because I'm trying to make them look better than they really are, but because it's impossible to do otherwise: the amount of tax you'll need to pay on the income from any given property will depend on whether you own the property as an individual or a company, your other earnings, your losses or expenditure across the rest of your portfolio, and plenty of other factors.

Just because it's impossible to generalise about the tax implications of any particular purchase, that doesn't mean it's not important: it's *very important indeed*. If you're new to property investment, you might be surprised by just how harsh the treatment of property income can be. While it's much more fun to get excited about the money you can make than to think about the money that could be taken away from you, you should absolutely spend plenty of time getting to grips with the tax implications of property investment before you begin. The time you spend structuring your investments to be as tax-efficient as possible at the beginning could add up to tens of thousands of pounds over your investing lifetime.

We'll cover the major aspects of tax you need to know in Part 2, so feel free to skip ahead and read that first if you want to. In the meantime I'll attempt to flag up the points at which it's an important consideration without getting into too much detail.

And finally, because my crystal ball's a bit hazy at the moment, I've been forced to lay everything out as if there aren't going to be any major changes in legislation – and who knows what might happen in terms of inflation, interest rates and everything else that affects an investment. That's why, again, these aren't intended to be 100% accurate and they're certainly not recommendations for what to do – just models to give you an idea of some of the different approaches that are out there.

I think that's enough caveats for now. Just one last thing before getting to the strategies: a quick overview of the calculations you'll encounter as we discuss the results of different investments.

Measuring success

To be successful in property investment, you need to know your numbers. I appreciate the beauty of a good spreadsheet as much as the next person (as long as the next person is extremely geeky too), but in truth, maths isn't my strong point. That's why I like to stick to three simple calculations, each of which is most useful in a slightly different situation.

You should already be familiar with these if you've read any other property books (including my one, Property Investment For Beginners). But as they crop up so often throughout this book, it's worth a quick refresher to make sure we're clear on exactly what we're talking about.

(As a quick note to avoid confusion, these calculations are always made on *pre-tax* returns for reasons discussed earlier.)

You'll hear a lot about yield, of which there are two types: **gross** and **net**. In general, when someone says "yield" and doesn't specify which type, they're talking about gross yield – and that's a convention I stick to here.

Gross yield is the annual rental income generated by an asset, divided by the price of acquiring it – so a property that brings in £10,000 per year in rent and cost you £100,000 to buy gives a gross yield of 10%. (On your calculator, that's 10,000 divided by 100,000. The result is 0.1, which expressed as a percentage is 10%.)

It clearly doesn't reflect the real results you'll get from an investment, because it doesn't take into account the costs you'll incur. As a result, saying "I got a gross yield of 10%" isn't enough to know whether that's a good thing or not – but because it's so simple to calculate, it's a handy rough-and-ready way to quickly compare properties that are likely to have similar costs associated with them.

(When I calculate gross yield, I like to include any major refurbishment costs in the "price of acquiring" part of the equation. After all, it's a bit misleading to calculate figures on the basis of buying a property for £70,000 if it's such a wreck that you immediately need to spend £30,000 doing it up.)

Net yield is the annual rental *profit* (rather than income) generated by an asset, divided by the price of acquiring it.

So if the property cost you £100,000, the annual rent is £10,000, and you have costs (including mortgage costs, management fees and maintenance) of £5,000, that's a net yield of 5%.

As this calculation takes costs into account, it's more useful than gross yield in situations where you can reliably estimate what your expenses will be. When different people talk about "net yield" you can never be totally sure which expenses they've accounted for – the big ones are obvious, but you could get down to the cost of shoe leather when walking over to inspect the property if you wanted to. It doesn't particularly matter: the calculations you make are only for yourself, so it's important just to be consistent with what you include so you're always comparing like with like.

Gross and net yield have their uses, but neither of them captures the entire investment equation. What we really need is a calculation that takes *everything* into account – and which we can use not just to compare different properties, but also to compare our return from a property investment to the returns we could get if we invested in a different asset class entirely.

That calculation is **Return on investment (ROI)** – calculated as the annual rental profit divided by *the money you put in*. If you buy wholly in cash, the money you put in is the same as the cost of acquiring the asset, so your ROI and net yield will be identical. But if you use a mortgage, your ROI will be higher than your net yield.

For example, take a property that cost £100,000 and generates a £3,000 annual profit after all costs – including the interest cost of a mortgage, which allowed you to borrow £75,000 so you only put in £25,000 of your own money. Your ROI is the £3,000 profit divided by the £25,000 cash you put in, which equals 12%.

You'd be forgiven for asking, "What's a good ROI?". Unfortunately, that's an almost impossible question to answer. But let me try.

It's easy to say what a *bad* ROI is: a negative one, meaning you're losing money. Beyond that, it's completely personal. For example, an ROI of 2% doesn't appeal to me – from such a low base, it doesn't take too many unexpectedly higher costs to turn things negative. But if you were particularly excited about a property's capital growth potential, maybe you wouldn't mind.

At the other end of the scale, some investors target ROIs of 20% or more – far beyond what I aim for. That's because they've got a strategy that's geared towards sweating their assets hard, perhaps by buying cheap houses and renting them out by the room. They know from experience that it's possible to achieve those returns with the model they follow, so they're not going to settle for less.

What should you be targeting? I'm not going to say, because there's no meaningful universal benchmark. Any number I throw out might on the one hand hold you back by giving you low expectations, and on the other put you off buying something that would have matched your goals perfectly because you're trying to hit the bottom of an arbitrary range. You should also be mistrustful of the numbers that other people quote (especially if they're trying to sell you something), because it's often hard to be sure what they're including. For example, the exact same property might give an ROI of 12% if you're self-managing, 8% if you're factoring in an agent's fees, or 5% if you've also put in more of your own cash because you want a smaller mortgage.

It's also worth noting that the ROI number is very sensitive to your borrowing cost. This is another reason someone else's claimed ROI is unhelpful, because you won't necessarily be able to borrow at the same rate they can. In the examples that follow, I've erred towards over-estimating the interest costs based on current rates, but your own rates will depend on your experience, the size of your portfolio, whether you're buying in a company structure, the nature of the property you're buying, the tenant demographic you're targeting, and so on. We'll get into this in a lot more detail at the start of Part 2.

Chapter 1

Save hard, take it easy, retire well

Aim: build a healthy income stream over 20 years without working too hard

In a nutshell: invest enough to buy one high-yielding property every 18 months, then increase the pace as rental income compounds

Upfront capital required: moderate

Effort involved: low initially, moderate as portfolio grows

Ongoing investment required: high

Payoff: long term

For this first strategy, we'll take the most basic form of property investment possible: saving up hard, and using those savings to buy properties. As time goes on you add each property's rental income to your savings, allowing you to pick up the pace.

You're not going to get rich off the income from one property, so this isn't a lot of use if you're desperate to quit your job right now (don't worry if that's you – we've got strategies to cover that later). Instead, this would work nicely if you're in your 30s or 40s, have a job that you enjoy, but don't fancy the idea of working until you're in your 60s or beyond.

At this stage in life it's common to have a demanding job and a young family, so you may want a strategy that doesn't involve putting in a lot of time or acquiring all sorts of specialist knowledge. This first strategy fits the bill nicely, but to compensate for the lack of time and skill needed, you *will* need to put in a fair bit of cash.

How much cash? Well, in the example I'm going to run you through below, you'll need to invest £30,000 to buy each property. If that sounds like a lot to save up… well, it is – if you wanted to buy one every 18 months, it's £1,666 per month. If you have a post-tax salary of £60,000, that's getting on for a third of your income.

If saving that much is impossible, you can tweak the variables by buying cheaper properties or waiting longer between purchases – but however you crack it, it's still a relatively capital-intensive strategy. In its favour though, it's *incredibly* safe and simple.

Let's get on to an example then – and assume that we've already saved up £30,000 to start off with.

Example

For the purposes of this example, we're going to Arnold, just north of Nottingham city centre. I've chosen it because (with no disrespect intended to the good people of Arnold) it's entirely unremarkable. It's not the most sought-after of areas, but you wouldn't avoid it after dark. It's not slap-bang in the city centre, but it has good transport links. And it's in the Midlands, so you know I've not chosen a remote former mining town in the North East just to make the numbers work. There are plenty of places just like Arnold all over the country.

In Arnold, to make a purchase work comfortably with a cash pot of less than £30,000, we're restricted to two-bedroom flats (although with a bit of negotiation, you *might* be able to get a two-bedroom house at the top end of your budget). A Rightmove search brings up plenty of flats in the £90,000–£100,000 price range that wouldn't need any refurbishment before renting. To demonstrate that success doesn't depend on getting the deal of the century, I'm selecting one at £95,000 and assuming we're just going to call the estate agent and buy it at the asking price with no attempt at negotiation.

In terms of the purchase then, the figures look like this:

- Deposit: £23,750 (25% of £95,000 purchase price)

- Purchase fees (solicitor, survey, broker fees, etc.): £1,500

- Stamp duty: £2,850 (for all examples, I'm using the higher rate of stamp duty that adds a 3% surcharge if you own another property already)

- Safety certificates and any odds and ends: £1,000

That's £28,100 spent, with enough savings left over to make sure we've got a bit of a buffer in case there are unexpected expenses before the rent starts piling up. Now, what about income?

Conveniently, the listing I'm looking at is being offered with tenants already in situ, and it tells me they're paying £625 per month. Looking at other listings locally, this seems a bit low: maybe they've been living there for a while and haven't had a rent increase. Nevertheless, let's go with it: I don't know the local market so it's best to be on the safe side.

Out of that £625, we need to account for the following monthly expenses:

- Mortgage (£71,250 borrowed on an interest-only basis at 4% interest): £237.50

- Service charge and ground rent: £58
(This is given on the listing I'm looking at, but annoyingly it often isn't – so it's a good idea to call the agent and ask before you get too excited.)

- Letting agent's property management fee at 10%: £62.50
  (You might decide to self-manage, in which case you won't have this management fee to pay. But to keep all these examples consistent, I'll include a typical management fee of 10% of the rent so that we're always comparing like with like.)

- Allowance for repairs at 10%: £62.50
  (Everyone has their own opinions about how much to allow for repairs, and I'd consider 10% for an apartment to be very high because many expenses are taken care of within the service charge. But, as above, I'm keeping my assumptions consistent throughout all the examples so that we're always comparing like with like.)

That leaves us with a monthly profit of £204.50.

Before calculating the annual profit, I'll assume that the property will be empty for two weeks per year. For a flat like this, I could imagine there being a month-long changeover every couple of years (allowing time to get in and do some maintenance too), but a fortnight every year is possible too.

After building that into the figures, we end up with an annual profit of £2,361.43 – which I'll round down to £2,200 to be extra cautious (and make the maths easier). Based on the £28,100 we put in, that represents an ROI of 8.4%.

That's the first purchase out of the way, and there's nothing left to do: all we've done is pop onto Rightmove, bought a property at the asking price, done no refurbishment beyond a quick tidy-up and handed it straight to a letting agent. Job done, and in rolls the rental income!

At its simplest, we can just repeat this exercise every 18 months. Do it for 15 years in a row, and we've got a rental income (ignoring tax) of roughly £22,000. After 30 years, we've got £44,000.

In fact, we can actually buy *more* properties as time goes on: in addition to our investment, we'll have the rent stacking up in our bank account. And while £2,200 in annual profit doesn't sound like much, it adds up quickly.

If we ignore tax again for a minute, the profits going into our bank account each year would be £2,200 in Year 1, £3,300 in Year 2, £4,400 in Year 3, and so on. By Year 6, we'd be able to buy *two* properties: one with the regular investment, and one with the accumulated years of rental income. By Year 15, we'd be able to buy two properties *every year*.

(It's worth noting that I've been talking in "today's money", but in reality there would be inflation to contend with. House prices, wages and rents will increase significantly over a decade or more, and this could be good or bad for your plans depending on by how much, and when, each of them grows. There are just too many variables to talk about it sensibly, so we'll stick to today's figures – while recognising the need to re-evaluate our strategy as time goes on and things change.)

In reality, tax will slow this pace down – although as we'll see when we come to the "Tax and accounting" section, your tax liability during the acquisition phase could well be lower than you think. Tax or no tax, once the snowball reaches a certain size, the momentum is hugely powerful: while at first it looks like it's going to take 30 years to accumulate 20 properties, it should actually be possible to get there in closer to 20 years by re-investing the profits.

Lessons

This example shows us the power of using leverage in the form of a mortgage – which we can see by comparing this strategy to a couple of alternatives.

By the time we've bought ten properties, we'll have invested £280,000 and generated an income of £22,000 per year. If we'd saved up until we could buy properties in cash instead of using mortgages, we'd have only been able to buy two properties – which would give an income of £10,300. On the face of it, using leverage has more than doubled the returns – but it's actually better than that. Firstly, buying instantly instead of saving up for extra years has brought in thousands of pounds of extra rental income. Also, if property prices go up by 10%, we've got ten properties that will increase in value (for a total gain of £95,000) instead of two (a total gain of £19,000).

(Using leverage has its risks too, and those mortgages will need to be paid off at some point – but those concerns are less significant than you might think. We'll talk about this a lot more in Part 2.)

Alternatively, if we'd invested that £280,000 in the stock market and later withdrawn it at a rate of 4% per year (a figure that many people claim is a "safe" withdrawal rate in retirement), we'd only end up with £11,200 per year.

This nicely demonstrates how powerful property investment can be, even if you do nothing special. Remember:

- I've barely mentioned the potential for the properties to increase in value. The property I chose for the example is in a popular owner-occupier area, so should deliver at least some degree of capital growth over the long term. This gives you interesting options in terms of building your portfolio faster or planning your exit strategy… of which, much more later in the book.

- The level of rent this property can achieve relative to its purchase price is relatively high, but it didn't require any special knowledge or hours of hunting to find.

- You're paying the asking price rather than negotiating any kind of discount.

- You're not doing any kind of refurbishment that would add value.

- There are no effort-intensive but higher cashflowing investments, like multi-lets.

- There's nothing clever at all, in fact. You just have to make one very standard purchase every 18 months, and nothing else.

There is, of course, one big assumption here: that you can afford to take large chunks of your earnings every year to finance the growth of your portfolio. For many people this isn't realistic, which is why the next strategy won't have this requirement. But the current strategy is a great "worst case" place to start, because it involves virtually no time or skill – so as your confidence increases, you can progress to other strategies that are less capital-intensive.

Whether you generate the funds by cutting your spending or increasing your earnings (or a combination), it's certainly not *easy*, but nor should it feel impossible – and the rewards are huge. Even if you hadn't invested in property at all you'd still be doing better than almost everyone else by saving up that much cash; leveraged property investment just pours petrol on the fire.

In this model, then, property isn't a get-rich-quick scheme or a method of generating huge returns in itself – which would be impossible with just one, pretty average, acquisition every 18 months. The magic is in the stealthy approach of combining property investment with living a restrained financial life. It's an approach that might leave you short on skiing holidays and

Gucci handbags, but *will* have your colleagues scratching their heads when you triumphantly hand in your notice 20 years before they could hope to do so…

Chapter 2

"Recycle" your cash

Aim: build an income stream while limiting the amount of capital you need to invest

In a nutshell: find properties that need refurbishing, do the work that will increase their value, and refinance so you need less of your own cash to put into the next purchase

Upfront capital required: moderate

Effort involved: moderate

Ongoing investment required: low

Payoff: medium term

After reading Strategy 1, you might be about to hurl this book down in disgust. "So you're telling me that if I just invest a shedload of money every year for the next 20 years, I'll be rich? I don't need a book to tell me that!"

Well, it's called property *investment* for a reason: you can't expect to make money without putting at least some resources in. But never fear: there are ways to get results even with a smaller cash input. In return though, you'll need to work a bit harder.

The strategy we'll look at next is sometimes known as "recycling your cash", because you reduce the amount of cash you need by taking one deposit and re-using it for multiple purchases. How? By *refurbishing* and *refinancing*.

Example

To keep things simple, let's take the same type of property in the same area of Nottingham where we bought for £95,000 as part of the previous strategy. But instead of paying £95,000, we find a flat that's near-identical other than being in pretty poor condition. We manage to negotiate buying that tired and unloved property for £65,000, then spend £10,000 bringing it back up to standard – thereby reinstating its "true" value of £95,000. Effectively we're creating £20,000 of equity out of thin air, which is our reward for improving its condition.

You might think that if a property needs £10,000 spending on it in order to raise its value to £95,000, you'll need to pay £85,000 for it. In fact, any investor would want some kind of "margin" as their reward for doing the work – otherwise they could just buy one that's already in good condition and save a lot of effort. The question is how far below £85,000 you can secure the property for, because that determines the size of the margin you build in.

Margin is hardest to find when the market is buoyant or supply is constrained, because an increase in competition or a lack of other options will mean that investors are willing to accept a smaller reward for doing the work. Later in the book we'll look at where to go looking for this kind of opportunity, but for now you'll need to take my word that it's *possible* but certainly not *easy*.

"Equity out of thin air" is the key to putting less cash into subsequent deals. Let's see how…

We'll start by buying the property for £65,000, but we won't use a mortgage to do so. A mortgage wouldn't be appropriate here, because:

- As you'll see, we only want this original loan for a matter of months, at which point we'll *refinance*. Mortgages are intended to be held for multiple years – so even if you use a mortgage product that doesn't have a specific penalty for paying it back early, lenders don't like it and might not lend to you again.

- A mortgage company might not lend anyway if they don't consider the property to be "habitable" – such as there being no functioning kitchen or bathroom, or the property just generally needing so much work that they don't think anyone could live there right now.

So a mortgage won't work, but we don't want to put in that much cash either. Instead, we'll use *bridging finance* – a form of short-term funding (usually up to a year), which is specifically intended for this kind of situation. Whereas mortgages are typically for up to 75% of the property's value, bridging normally goes up no further than 70%. It's more expensive than a mortgage – the interest rate is usually in the range of 0.75%–1.5% per month, plus fees of around 2% of the total loan amount – but it's quick and easy to arrange.

(The terms of bridging loans – the rates payable, and when and how fees are paid – vary extensively between different lenders. To provide a "worst case" for this example, I'm assuming that you need to pay all the interest and fees out of your own pocket at the outset. In reality, the terms will be more favourable to you than that.)

Let's look at the purchase:

- Deposit: £19,500 (30% of £65,000 purchase price, with a £45,500 bridging loan for the rest)

- Stamp duty: £1,950

- Finance costs: £4,095 (based on a borrowing rate of 1% per month for eight months, plus a 2% fee)

- Refurb cost: £10,000

- Purchase fees (solicitor, survey, broker, etc.): £1,500

Add this all together, and we'll need to put in £37,045. It's more than the straightforward buy-to-let purchase from Strategy 1 involved, but don't worry – we'll be getting a lot of it back soon. (And as I've said, in reality the finance can be structured to put in less cash upfront.)

Now, once the work has been done, we'll want to get off our expensive bridging loan and onto a traditional mortgage product. And importantly, when we do so, we want to borrow 75% of the *new* value of the property (i.e. the £95,000 we believe it's now worth rather than the £65,000 we paid for it).

Under most circumstances, you can't apply to re-finance until you've owned the property for six months (which is why I allowed for eight months of bridging payments), so we put a tenant in the property while we wait for that day to arrive. When it does, we borrow 75% of £95,000 – which leaves our cash position like this:

- New borrowing (75% of £95,000 valuation): £71,250

- Repay bridging loan: £45,500

- Left in the bank: £25,750

We originally invested £37,045 and got £25,750 back after refinancing – meaning we now have just £11,295 tied up in that property. If we want to move on to another identical purchase, we already have £25,750 in the bank – so we just need to save up that extra £11,295 in order to do the exact same thing again.

Before moving on to discuss the implications of this, let's see what our month-to-month finances look like now we're refinanced. Again, the rental income is £625.

- Mortgage payment (interest-only loan of £71,250 at 4% interest rate): £237.50

- Service charge and ground rent: £58

- Management fee at 10%: £62.50

- Allowance for repairs at 10%: £62.50

That leaves us with a monthly profit of £204.50.

Like last time, I'm going to build in an allowance for the property being empty for two weeks out of every year. After doing so, that leaves us with an annual pre-tax profit of £2,361.43 – which again I'll knock down to £2,200 to be on the safe side.

In profit terms, that's identical to Strategy 1 – where we just bought the property for its market value. When you look at our ROI though, things are very different. On the straight purchase for its market value, it was 7.8%. After buying cheap, refurbishing and refinancing, it's 19.4%. That makes sense: we're making the same *return* on a smaller *investment* left in after refinancing.

Lessons

So, where does this leave us?

Well, it leaves us needing to find less than £12,000 to invest again. That means that if we manage to save "just" £1,000 per month, we can buy one property every year. (And, just like before, by saving up the rental income it will soon accumulate and allow us to buy at a faster rate.)

As a result, by putting in more effort in terms of finding the opportunity and doing the refurbishment, we're able to put ourselves in exactly the same position as in Strategy 1 while halving the cash requirement. (Noting, of course, that the *initial* cash requirement is higher because we can't borrow quite as much and need to find the funds to pay for the refurbishment.) If we'd managed to secure a bigger discount, it would have been possible to do even better (it's theoretically possible to get *all* your cash back out of a deal upon refinancing – although admittedly it's not easy).

Here we see what's going to be a common theme in this book: when you've got less cash to invest, you'll have to put in more effort and accept more risk to get the same result. And vice versa.

We haven't addressed the risk in this strategy yet, so let's do that now. Whereas with a straight "purchase and wait" strategy you can't go far wrong, successfully executing a "buy-refurbish-refinance" strategy involves:

- Finding the opportunity in the first place

- Accurately judging the refurbishment cost, so you know how much you can afford to pay for the property and still get the margin you need

- Successfully negotiating the purchase at that price

- Conducting the refurbishment on time and on budget

- Convincing the mortgage lender's valuer that the property is, mere months later, worth significantly more than you paid for it

Later in the book we'll see how to do all of these things. But at every one of these points there's not only more effort to be made, but also an element of risk to accept. Even the most experienced investor gets things wrong occasionally.

There's also risk associated with short-term market changes. For example, if the market drops 20% while you're in the process of adding 20% in value, you won't be able to get the revaluation you were hoping for. Over the course of a long-term investment, these dips can be ridden out (if you structure your portfolio to survive a recession, which we'll discuss in Part 3), but it'll affect your plans more drastically if it happens at the wrong time while you're trying to lock in a gain.

Before wrapping up, let's just cover a couple of points to help generalise this strategy to situations other than the one I've presented here.

Firstly, if you're able to fund the initial purchase and refurbishment with your own cash instead of using a bridging loan, all the better: you'll save on some hefty fees. (Although there's an "opportunity cost" to consider if you could have been doing something else useful with that money.)

Another advantage of cash is that you're not *forced* to refinance as quickly as possible to get yourself off the expensive bridging finance rates. If the market did take a temporary tumble at the wrong time – or for some other reason it turned out to take longer before you could refinance – you could just wait it out without worrying about your interest rate.

Secondly, don't be put off by the fact that I've used a relatively cheap property as an example in this strategy. It works every bit as well on more expensive properties – and can work anywhere in the country. I've only stuck to the example of a cheap property because it allows you to buy one per year with an amount of savings that won't seem outrageous to most people. If you're able to invest more, or you're willing to wait a couple of years or more between purchases, everything I've said applies to pricier properties too.

Chapter 3

Lock away a lump sum and watch it grow

Aim: invest a lump sum of cash, and turn it into a much larger amount of cash (or a mortgage-free income) in 10–20 years

In a nutshell: buy properties with an eye on capital growth, then sit back and wait

Upfront capital required: high

Effort involved: low

Ongoing investment required: low

Payoff: long term

So far, we've looked at two strategies that only take into account one source of property profits – rental income – without really mentioning the possibility of capital growth. Let's put that right.

Firstly, back to basics. With any property you buy, you have two potential sources of "return" on that investment:

- Profit left over after receiving the rent and paying out your expenses

- Growth in the property's value over time

When some people calculate their "ROI", they combine their rental profits with a *projected* percentage uplift in capital growth every year. Personally, I don't see the sense in this: for a start it doesn't reflect reality (there's no way property will go up by exactly the same steady percentage every year), and also that increase in value doesn't do you any good until you either sell or refinance to access the extra equity.

I don't want to give you the idea that capital growth isn't important: in many cases, the returns you get from capital growth will dwarf the rental income you receive. But capital growth isn't *certain*, whereas rental profits are. As an investor, you'll therefore be looking at properties that target some mixture of the two – and you can be strategic in your acquisitions to target properties that are more heavily weighted towards one or the other. In the first two strategies we focused 100% on income, and treated any capital growth as a bonus. In this strategy, we'll go completely the other way.

Example

In this example we'll pretend we've got £250,000 burning a hole in our bank account, ready to be invested in property. This strategy is just as applicable when you're investing smaller amounts of money, with the caveat that low-value properties (to pluck a very rough number out of the air, I'd say under £70,000) tend not to offer the greatest growth potential. This is an idea we'll return to later.

£250,000 might sound like a lot of money to have saved up – and it is – but you'd be surprised by how many people I hear from who have that kind of sum to invest. Alternatively, some of that cool quarter mil' might be in the form of equity that you can take out of your own home. That's fine (as long as you have the income to support the extra borrowing), but bear in mind that you'll have higher personal mortgage payments to meet each month and/or be extending the amount of time until your home is paid off.

By definition, a strategy that prioritises capital growth is going to be a medium-to-long-term strategy – so for the purposes of this example we're interested in where a £250,000 investment can get us in 20 years' time.

As we've seen, mortgages are typically available for up to 75% of the property's value. With our £250,000, then, we could theoretically buy £1 million of property – although it will actually end up being slightly less because there'll be transaction fees to account for (legal fees, stamp duty and so on).

While that money *could* buy one mansion with its own home cinema and climate-controlled wine room, it would turn out to be a terrible (if fun) investment. Instead, it would be more wise to split that investment between five properties worth around £170,000 each.

For this example, we'll travel down to Southampton and go shopping for a nice, modern two-bedroom flat in the SO15 postcode area.

By just going in and paying the full asking price with no attempt at negotiation, we can make a ready-to-rent purchase for £170,000. The purchase costs break down like this:

- Deposit: £42,500 (25% of £170,000 purchase price)

- Stamp duty: £6,000

- Purchase fees (solicitor, survey, broker, etc.): £1,500

That's a total investment of £50,000. Repeat five times (I'm assuming all at the same time to keep the maths easy, but you can space them out of course), and that's our £250,000 neatly spent.

A two-bedroom flat in this area should rent for around £900 per month. From that £900, we'll deduct the following running costs:

- Mortgage payment (£127,500 borrowed interest only at 4%): £425

- Service charge and ground rent: £100 (estimated)

- Management at 10%: £90

- Repairs allowance at 10%: £90

After allowing for the property being empty for two weeks per year, we get to a monthly profit of £187.64.

With five of these, that gives us a grand total of £938 per month before tax. Life-changing? Absolutely not, but that's not what we're interested in for the purposes of this strategy.

Instead, join me in my time machine as we travel 20 years into the future – by which point presumably estate agents have been replaced by robots, you can download the contents of this book directly onto a chip in your brain, and U2 is still putting out disappointing albums. We've handed all our properties over to a letting agent, and barely given them a second thought. When we finally remember to check up on them, where have we ended up?

At this point I'll make a statement that might sound like a huge assumption, but I think is actually a very safe bet: property prices will have at least doubled after 20 years.

Historically, property prices in the UK have doubled on average every nine years (the longest doubling period has been 14 years). Now, we need to be very careful about two things: extrapolating forward from historical data, and applying a UK average to a specific situation. We'll come back to both these points, but for now we can be somewhat confident that by extending the timeframe to 20 years, doubling will have occurred.

So, in 20 years our five properties – worth a combined £850,000 when we bought them – will be worth £1.7 million. Yet, brilliantly, the total borrowing will be exactly the same as it was before: £637,500. This is the magic of leverage once again: while property prices and rents go up over the long term (even if only in line with inflation), the amount borrowed stays the same. (Of course, the *interest rate* on that borrowing can change – which is why you need room in your figures to incur higher borrowing costs without being in a loss-making situation. Expect to see lots more about this in Part 3.)

At this point, we have at least two options.

The first option is to sell them all. After paying off the mortgages, we'll have just over £1m in the bank. We don't know what the capital gains tax (CGT) regime of the future will be, but if we assume it's the same as it is now and we don't take even the most basic measures to mitigate it, we'll be left with £700,000 after tax.

So we originally put in £250,000, and got out £700,000. What would your options be if you'd followed this formula and ended up with this sum? Depending on your age and your plans, you can choose to gradually spend it to cover your expenses for the rest of your life, put it into other investments, or even re-invest it into more properties. Let's say you don't want to use mortgages for your next round of purchases, so you buy them all in cash and achieve an ROI of 4% per year. That will give you an annual income of £28,000.

Alternatively, you could sell one of the properties to release £212,500 in cash. Even after paying CGT, that'll be nearly enough to pay off the mortgages on two of the others – so let's chuck in a small amount of the rental profits that we'd almost forgotten had been accumulating for 20 years (and will now be more than £200,000 pre-tax) to clear those two mortgages completely.

That leaves us with four properties, two of which are mortgage-free. As a result of paying off those mortgages, your monthly profit across the remaining four has increased to £1,615. That's £19,380 per year – and you've still got four properties that will keep growing in value, with a very conservative level of debt (the loan-to-value across the portfolio is just under 19%, which could easily be paid off with another sale or accumulated rental income whenever you wanted).

The great thing about rental income is that rents tend to rise in line with inflation over time – so whatever income you're deriving from whatever property you keep on holding, you'll theoretically keep being paid the "real terms" equivalent of that amount forever.

Lessons

Other than demonstrating the power of time on leveraged property investment (and giving capital growth some attention after we'd ignored it in previous strategies), the purpose of this example was to get you thinking about *where* and *what* you buy.

Let's start with "where". I said that, historically, prices in the UK have doubled on average every nine years. But you're not going to approximate the "average" unless you own hundreds of properties in every part of the UK – so if you're interested in capital growth, location matters.

I don't necessarily mean that you should search for the elusive "hotspot" where prices will outperform everywhere else in the UK. Instead, you just need to look out for parts of the UK where you can take a reasonable punt on growth being stronger overall than other areas. For example, cities will as a rule experience more growth than more sparsely populated areas because they're the economic hubs where jobs are created as the economy expands. And in terms of industry and investment, you'd bet that parts of the country like the North East are going to struggle more than the South East or North West. (A decade or two is a long time to turn things around, of course, but we can only really work with what we know to be true today.)

I chose Southampton pretty much at random when I was trying to think of an economically strong city that's likely to continue doing well – but there are any number of other cities I could have chosen. In fact, I'd prefer to choose more of them and (in the previous example) own one flat in five different cities: it reduces the odds of finding a massive winner, but I'm also less likely to have put all my eggs in a basket that underperforms.

"Where to buy" applies to the location *within* cities too, and intersects with "what to buy". As a rule, growth happens first and fastest in prime and central areas. That's why I chose in my example to use a modern, relatively new flat in a popular area. The monthly return would have been a lot higher if I'd chosen a house on the fringes (there wouldn't have been a service charge, and the purchase price would have been lower relative to the rent), but the intention was to maximise capital growth potential. When the economy is in full swing and growth is in the air, demand is always going to be highest (and therefore push up the price more) for the best properties in the best locations. Over the course of 20 years, that can make a huge difference to capital growth.

This is the yield/growth trade-off that we often see: as a general rule, properties that achieve higher yields (relative to the area in general) will experience capital growth later and less strongly. I've somewhat simplified things, because if a property's yield is *temporarily* higher than one would expect for that kind of property, buyers will be attracted and prices will rise to remove the discrepancy. We'll come back to this when we discuss the property cycle in Part 3, but for now just be aware that you'll generally need to choose a property with some kind of yield/growth compromise in mind.

Finally, I've not mentioned "when to buy". When property prices double, they don't just drift upwards in a nice predictable way. The majority of that growth happens in just a few years, and is immediately followed by some of the gains being rapidly lost. This is the phenomenon of the property cycle, which we'll cover in a lot of detail in Part 3 – because if capital growth is your objective, it's a big part of the picture. You should never truly put the blinkers on for 20 years (as in our example) because then you're just leaving to chance whether you end up selling at a good time or a bad time. I'd love to get into the property cycle in more detail now, but I'll restrain myself. Trust me, it's exciting stuff – think of it as your reward for trudging through some of the drearier bits about accounting that we need to get into later.

Chapter 4

Replace your wage with rent- al income – fast

Aim: turn cash in the bank into an income stream that allows you to quit your job as quickly as possible

In a nutshell: buy a small number of properties that generate a lot of cash immediately

Upfront capital required: high

Effort involved: high, if self-managing

Ongoing investment required: low

Payoff: short term

All of the strategies we've looked at so far have had a relatively long-term payoff. That's all well and good (and time is where a lot of the magic of property happens), but what if you're thoroughly sick of your job and want to quit RIGHT NOW? Well, with this strategy (and the next one) we'll look at ways to create that instant income you need.

Both work best when you have a decent amount of capital to start with. This makes sense: if you have the luxury of time, you can put in more cash over the years or allow equity to build up. That's not an option if you need to generate a return on your money from day one.

This particular strategy is all about accumulating rental income *fast* – which puts us squarely in the territory of multi-lets rather than single lets. When a property is rented out room by room, the total income generated by that property is generally higher – and of course, the more lettable rooms you can squeeze in (by converting reception rooms into bedrooms or sub-dividing large rooms), the more income you generate.

(A multi-let is also known as a House in Multiple Occupation (HMO), and we'll use the term HMO from here onwards. "HMO" is actually defined in several different ways for different purposes, and it's possible to have a multi-let that isn't an HMO... but that isn't important right now.)

The downside is that HMOs involve more management (in terms of keeping all the rooms occupied and making sure everyone is happy), and there will generally be higher maintenance costs as the house is being used more intensively. Let's look at a couple of examples that demonstrate all of these points. Just like in the previous strategy, we'll imagine that we've got £250,000 to invest.

Example 1

We'll start with the example of a mini-HMO in Liverpool, aimed at students.

Let's look at buying a two-bedroom terraced house in the student-y L7 postcode, where the reception room would be converted into a third bedroom. From a quick look on Rightmove, it seems you can buy one for around £60,000 in a not-ideal-but-passable location, then budget £10,000 to smarten it up a bit.

So the cash investment needed is:

- 25% deposit on £60,000 purchase price: £15,000

- Stamp duty: £1,800

- Refurbishment: £10,000

- Purchase fees (solicitor, survey, broker, etc.): £1,500

For a total investment of £28,300.

The house will have three lettable rooms, each of which should command a rent of £82 per week, for a monthly total rent roll of £1,065. That's a gross yield (dividing the annual rent by the total purchase price *and* refurbishment cost) of 18.2% – more than double the typical yield of a single family home.

But before you get too excited, it's worth remembering that HMOs come with more than their fair share of expenses too – so after factoring these in, your actual ROI won't look quite that exciting.

One big extra expense is bills, which in HMOs (unlike in single lets) are usually included as part of the rent: £20 per room per week is a fairly standard estimate for rooms let to professionals, although it may be lower for students because they're exempt from council tax. Management fees (if you don't plan to self-manage) are also generally higher, as more work is involved than a single let.

So from our gross monthly rent of £1,065 I'm going to deduct:

- Mortgage (£45,000 borrowed interest only at 5%): £187.50

- Insurance: £20 (not included in previous examples because insurance is usually covered by a flat's service charge)

- Bills (£20 per room per week): £259.80

- Repairs allowance of 10%: £106.50

- Management at 12.5% (typically higher than for single lets): £133.15

You'll notice that I've bumped the interest rate of the mortgage up a bit, because borrowing for HMOs tends to be more expensive.

That gets us to a monthly profit of £358.05, or an ROI of 15.2%. In fact, though, student lets tend to run for a period of 11 months – so by the time you allow for a month without income and average that out over the year, the monthly profit reduces to £280.40 and the ROI to 11.9%.

With our £250,000, we could buy nine of these (OK, we'd need to negotiate a discount of £5,000 across all nine properties to hit our budget), for a total monthly pre-tax income of £2,523.60. Enough to quit your job? It might be a pay cut, but even after factoring in time for admin and phone calls from your letting agent, you'd still have plenty of time on your hands to pursue other sources of income. If your thumbs started to hurt from all the twiddling and you wanted to self-manage, you'd save £1,200 per month and take your monthly income to over £3,700.

This all sounds great, but there are some drawbacks to take seriously.

Firstly, terraced houses in student areas tend not to be the most desirable, so (in accordance with what we've seen in previous examples) they're unlikely to give much in the way of capital growth. If you consider "total profit" (rental profit plus equity gain) over the entire time that you own the property, it could end up *lower* than a single let even though the month-to-month income is higher. This becomes even more marked when you divide your total profit by the number of hours you put in over the duration of the investment. Capital growth is never any kind of certainty, but you could end up making less money for more work, even though the ROI appears to be higher.

Another downside, when it comes to student HMOs at least, is concentration of risk. What you've basically got here are cheap, not-that-great houses that students happen to be willing to pay a good chunk of cash to live in right now. If trends shift (as they're doing in many student areas towards purpose-built accommodation), you could suddenly be the proud owner of nine unexciting houses where your yield has just been cut in half and your tenants have recurring cameos on Crimewatch.

Example 2

The "trend-shift risk" we saw in the previous example is specific to a particular type of student property, though. The HMO sector in general is thriving and should continue to do so, because young people aren't going to find it any easier to afford their own flats – even to rent. So in the professional market you've got people living in rented accommodation well into their 30s, and in the housing benefit market you've got people who are only given enough to cover a room rather than a flat until they're 35 (unless they have dependents).

Let's take another example then, because owning nine houses seems like a lot of work and there are risks involved. Could you quit your job by just owning a handful of more upmarket professional house shares that are less at risk of a drop in rental demand?

Here's a real-life example from a friend in the Midlands:

- Purchase price: £190,000

- Stamp duty: £7,000

- Refurb and set-up: £10,000

- Number of bedrooms: 6

- Rent per room per month: £370

- Total income: £2,220

- Total bills: £500 (including insurance – just under the £20 per room per week figure that I estimated earlier)

- Mortgage: £593 (£142,500 borrowed interest only at 5%)

- Repairs allowance of 10%: £220

This gives an ROI of 16.84% and a monthly profit after costs of £905. £250,000 would just about buy four of these (with a fractional discount or saving on a refurb), giving an income of £3,620 per month.

You can't tell from the example, but it wasn't easy to pack six bedrooms into that house. The chap who gave me the case study is a dab hand at reconfiguring houses to squeeze in as many rooms as possible without making it overly pokey or breaching any regulations. This is where expertise comes in: if you thought it was only possible to get five bedrooms out of that house, your returns would have been cut dramatically.

The takeaway lesson from this scenario? That you can buy four houses, generate £3,620 per month and potentially quit your job. However, you've just given yourself multiple *new* jobs: you're now a letting agent, general dogsbody, referee in fights over who got crumbs in the butter, and so on. While HMOs seem more profitable than single lets, some of that profit has a time cost attached to it – and while being a full-time landlord might sound more glamorous than the job you've got now, you could be pining for a nice easy office job after a few months of running around after multiple tenants.

The alternative is, of course, to use a managing agent – but doing so reduces the ROI to not far off what you'd expect from a single let. In the example above, adding in management at 12.5% would add £277.50 in costs for each house, or £1,110 in total. This reduces the monthly income to £2,518, and the ROI to 11.67%.

Actually, your costs of using an agent will be even higher be-cause most agents will charge a letting fee every time they rent a room on top of the management fee. If six rooms are turning over once per year and the agent charges £150 each time, that's another £75 monthly cost on average.

This example, therefore, brings out another truth of property investment: outsized returns are generally earned, through hard work and hard-won expertise. In the scenario above, if you do the management yourself (hard work) and know how to maximise the amount of rent you can generate from any given house (hard-won expertise), you'll do very well. Otherwise you'll have to settle for lower returns.

Not that there's anything wrong with either approach. You might be happy with making a lower return if you want to spend your time on other things and would rather outsource the management. Alternatively, you might prefer the job of being a part-time HMO manager to the job you've got right now – and you might even be able to systemise it, take on other people's properties and eventually employ someone to do the job for you.

Chapter 5

Flip your way out of the day job

Aim: embark on a new career as a property trader – bringing in enough money to replace your wage

In a nutshell: buy, fix up, and sell on for a profit

Upfront capital required: high for best results, but moderate can work too

Effort involved: high

Ongoing investment required: low

Payoff: short term

In the last strategy we looked at how to use a lump sum to create an income *right now*, so that you can get out of your job pronto. What if you still want to tell your boss where to stick it, but don't have that much cash to put to work?

To demonstrate this strategy, we'll use £50,000 as the amount of starting capital. This £50,000 won't be enough to buy a decent chunk of rental income, even with HMOs. Realistically then, the only way to get an immediate income is to look at *trading* in property (rather than *investing* in property): buying, refurbishing, and selling on at a higher price. "Trading", "buy-to-sell" and "flipping" are all used pretty much synonymously to refer to this process.

As you don't have enough to buy a property purely with cash, you can use bridging finance – which, as we saw earlier, is a handy but costly form of short-term lending. Alternatively, you could approach a friend or a family member who has cash in the bank and offer them a fixed percentage return on their money for the duration of the project. (You could instead offer to go in 50/50 with them and split the profits, but that's a worse deal for you unless they bring skills to the table too.)

Example

For this example we'll look at a property that we can buy for £90,000, and needs £18,000 spending on it in order to bring it into tip-top condition. Once it's gone from tired and unappealing to shiny and desirable, we reckon we can sell it for £140,000.

With bridging you can typically borrow 70% of the property's value, so we'll borrow £63,000 and put in £27,000 as a deposit. That means the upfront costs are:

- Deposit: £27,000 (30% of £90,000 purchase price)

- Stamp duty: £2,700

- Refurbishment budget: £18,000

- Purchase fees (solicitor, survey, broker, etc.): £1,500

So that's £49,200 of the £50,000 cash pot spent.

There will also be costs associated with the bridging loan of £63,000. It's usually possible to structure the loan so that these fees (or at least the majority of them) are paid at the end of the project, but in case of any upfront fees there's £800 left in the budget to cover them. I'm going to assume that we borrow the money for eight months, at an interest rate of 1% per month and with fees totalling 2% of the amount borrowed. That leaves total borrowing costs of £6,300 to pay back.

Because we're professionals, we run the project like a military operation and finish on time and on budget, finally achieving the anticipated sale price of £140,000. With the property sold, it's time to calculate the profit. The difference between the purchase price (£90,000) and sale price (£140,000) is £50,000 – from which we need to deduct:

- Refurbishment: £18,000

- Stamp duty: £2,700

- Bridging interest and fees: £6,300

- Legal fees and other transaction costs (for both purchase and sale): £3,000

That leaves a profit of £20,000.

I said I was going to leave tax aside for these models, but it's more straightforward to calculate with property trading: if the property was bought within a limited company (generally a good idea for buy-to-sell projects, as we'll see later), we'll pay corporation tax (currently 19%) on the profits. That would leave a post-tax profit from this project of £16,200.

In theory, if everything goes perfectly, six-month projects like this could be run back-to-back – allowing two to be completed per year. That would give the company £32,400 in post-tax profit, although, like with any company, there may be additional tax to pay when taking money out as a wage or as dividends.

So, ready to quit your job right now and start trading? I wouldn't recommend it – because even for people who are highly experienced, it's *never* the case that everything goes perfectly. If you end up with a property where everything goes wrong and you only break even, or which you can't sell at all and are stuck with, you're stuffed: your cash is tied up and you don't have enough money to pay the bills.

A more sensible approach would be to keep your job temporarily, and do some flips on the side to start with. If you can execute three successful flips like the one we've just been through, you've pretty much doubled your money – leaving the company with £48,600 post-tax to add to your original £50,000.

At that point (which could be less than two years away), you'll then have nearly £100,000 with which to kick off your career as a full-time flipper – meaning you can either run two projects at once, or (with a greater concentration of risk) trade in properties that are twice as expensive so you make twice as much profit for the same amount of effort.

Of course, if you have more cash to start with – or the contacts who are willing to lend you more money – you can be full-time from the start. But the point is that once you start living off your profits instead of re-investing them, you're more personally vulnerable to things going wrong: a house that takes twice as long as expected to sell isn't just annoyingly slowing down your plans – it's potentially affecting your ability to meet your personal financial obligations.

Lessons

The trading model is pretty *simple*, but that doesn't necessarily make it *easy*. Executing this successfully involves:

- Identifying the opportunities

- Arranging finance

- Acquiring the properties

- Correctly estimating the costs

- Running an on-time and on-budget refurbishment pro-ject (either by doing the work yourself or managing a team of contractors)

- Presenting the property correctly so that it sells at the price you need within the desired timeframe

… All while simultaneously looking out for the next one, so you can get started as soon as the cash comes back into your bank account. This only emphasises the point I made in the previous model: that rapid profits need to be earned through hard work or hard-won knowledge.

So it requires a fair bit of effort and successful execution, but as a means of escaping your job and getting full-time into property in a couple of years with only a modest amount of capital? It's not for everyone, but for the right kind of person it's likely to be a much more enjoyable way of making a living.

Conclusion

Excited? You should be – because although we've only looked at a few of the many possible strategies out there, you should be seeing how there's an approach to suit every goal, timescale, budget and skill set.

It's nearly time to move on to Part 2 and put the theory into action, so let's just quickly recap some of the general themes that we've encountered while looking at these strategies.

- The tighter the timescale to reach your goal or the smaller the amount of money you can put in at the start, the more hands-on you'll need to be, and the less certain you can be of getting your result. For example, if you're trying to generate immediate cash through trading property (Strategy 5) you'll have to work hard and there's a lot more that can go wrong than if you're just buying and collecting the rent over the years (Strategy 1). Appreciating this and understanding your constraints in these areas is the key to setting realistic goals.

- Each example I gave started with an investment of at least £25,000 – so what do you do if you have less than that? The obvious answer would be to save up, but you could also team up with a friend or family member who has the money. Later in the book we'll look at how to correctly structure a joint venture like this.

- What you buy and where you buy has a large impact on the relative contributions that *rental income* and *capital growth* make to your total returns. You can target investments that produce a strong rental return if that's your preference, or instead target those that are most likely to benefit from strong capital growth – and there will always be some degree of compromise. You'll continue to notice this as you start researching your own options in more detail.

- All the strategies described in this chapter involve very different skills, preferences and attitudes to risk. Coming up with your own plan is a matter of finding a strategy that matches not only your goals, but your personality too: there's no point working out a brilliant plan that involves flipping a house every six months if you work 18 hours per day in the City and have absolutely no interest in construction projects. Finding the sweet spot that matches up all these different factors isn't easy, but it's worth the effort of getting it right.

So, there you go – we've given a lot of thought to the final destination, which was vital to do before setting off. Between here and there, there's much to be done – starting with lining up the finance and finding a property to buy, and progressing all the way through the acquisition process to management and beyond. It's a lot of work, but it's (mostly) all good fun too – and Part 2 will cover all of it in detail.

PART 2:
THE INVESTMENT PROCESS

Introduction

With your strategy in place, we can turn to the mechanics of property investment: getting financing, deciding where to buy, analysing potential opportunities, then following the process all the way through to either management or sale. As a special treat, we can even talk about tax for a bit.

I wouldn't describe the process as "easy", because there's a lot to it and there are plenty of potential setbacks, but there's no one particular aspect where you need to be a genius. You'll find different parts of the process challenging depending on your strengths and weaknesses: some people really struggle to find good opportunities, others get bogged down in the research, and many find the management and record keeping to be a real chore.

Whatever your particular abilities though, this whole process becomes easier once you've got a strategy in place. For a start, it answers a lot of questions about the type of property you should be looking for – and therefore removes a good deal of uncertainty. It will also keep you motivated, because you'll know how worthwhile it will be once you've achieved your goals.

So, let's dive in – starting with the all-important financing of your investment…

Chapter 6

Finance

When I was in my teens and early twenties, I'd always read the "Money" section of the newspaper at the weekends. I couldn't get enough of anything to do with dividends, savings and interest rates... but I was never able to muster up any excitement for the (seemingly endless) articles about mortgages.

In truth, I don't think I fully understood what they were – I just knew they were scary, and that adults seemed to spend disproportionate amounts of time stressing out about them. I remember repeatedly thinking, "I'm never going to have one of those... I'll just wait until I have enough money of my own to buy a house outright."

Fast-forward a decade and, much like my "This Twitter lark seems like a silly fad" prediction of 2007, I turned out to be spectacularly wrong. I now have a number of mortgages – far more than the average "normal" person. Even more strangely, I actually find the whole business of finance totally fascinating.

Your view of debt is probably less warped than mine used to be, but you're still likely to have all sorts of hang-ups and uncertainties around mortgage lending (and its alternatives). This chapter is here to help.

By making this the first chapter of Part 2, I seem to be suggesting that you should consider how to fund a purchase before you even go out looking for something you might want to buy – why is that?

It's a common newbie mistake to rush out and look at properties, only to have to back out of a deal later because you can't borrow as much as you thought you could. It's a waste of your time, and it destroys your credibility with the estate agent you were dealing with. That's why I recommend understanding the basic factors that influence lending and looking into your options before you begin.

Focusing on finance first will give you (justified) confidence that you'll be able to go ahead when you find something suitable. It will also give you as much time as possible to address any factors that might restrict your ability to take on borrowing.

We'll start with the most basic question of all: if you have a decent amount of cash saved up, should you take out a mortgage at all?

Should you get a mortgage?

Say you have £50,000 sitting in your bank account. Should you buy one small terraced house in the cheapest part of town with that cash, or take out a mortgage to buy two bigger and more desirable houses for £100,000 each?

Answer: the latter. Almost always.

To explain why, let's say property prices go up by 10%. In the first scenario your portfolio has increased in value by £5,000, and in the second the value has increased by £20,000 – *even though your own cash investment is the same*. After a 10% increase in prices, you could theoretically sell both houses immediately and bank a 40% return on your investment (the £20,000 gain divided by your £50,000 cash input) – ignoring transaction fees and so forth.

That's leverage. As this simple example shows, it's exceptionally powerful – and it should be treated with the caution it deserves.

There are two dangers to be mindful of. First of all, leverage works against you when prices fall: if property values had dropped by 10% in our example, you would have *lost* 40% of your investment. This is only an issue, however, if you're forced to sell at that point. If you can ride out the dip and wait for prices to pick up again, you're all good. How do you make sure you can ride out the dips? By protecting your cashflow at all costs. If a property is making a profit, you should be able to hold on to it forever, through good times and bad.

However, the second danger is that having a mortgage *decreases* your cashflow (compared to if you bought with cash), because you have an extra cost to contend with: the cost of repaying the mortgage. This is why it's dangerous to be over-leveraged: if you have huge borrowings and interest rates go up (thus increasing your monthly payments), you could be stuck in a situation where the property is *costing* you money every month. If you run out of ability to subsidise the property at the same time as prices have just collapsed and you can't sell it for a high enough price to repay the mortgage... bad news. Like, "bankruptcy" bad.

(In Part 3 we'll look at property crashes and how to ensure you have a sufficient safety margin to survive in almost any circumstances.)

Despite the dangers, using leverage responsibly will still do wonderful things for your long-term returns. Unless your personal situation is such that you wouldn't be comfortable with any kind of debt, it's something you should strongly consider.

Deciding on interest only vs capital repayment

When taking out a mortgage on a buy-to-let property, you'll be able to choose between repaying a small amount of the loan each month until you owe nothing at the end of the mortgage term (a "capital repayment" loan), or just paying off the interest each month so that at the end of the term you still owe exactly as much as you borrowed in the first place (an "interest-only" loan).

If you're not overly comfortable with debt, capital repayment will seem like the "safe" choice. But I'm going to try to convince you that "interest only" is actually safer.

Why? Because if you're repaying a chunk of the capital each month, it means your monthly payments will be higher and your cashflow will therefore be lower. And, as we've already seen, the real danger is that you're stuck in a position where prices have crashed *and* the property is making a loss (because your rental income doesn't cover your expenses).

Paying off just the interest gives you more income each month. Yes, you need to find the money to repay the mortgage in the distant future when you're unable to extend the loan term any further – but you'll get a major helping hand from inflation.

Inflation is an extremely powerful force, but it's easy to miss because, year to year, it's barely noticeable. Over a 25-year mortgage term though, its effect is huge. Let's say you borrow £75,000 today (to buy a house worth £100,000) and pay off nothing but the interest. Assuming annual inflation of just 2%, its "real value" by the time you pay it back in 25 years will be only £45,000. At the same time, let's assume house prices increase by 2% per year too – so the house you bought for £100,000 will be worth £164,000 in 25 years.

As a result, even though you haven't paid off a penny of the amount you borrowed, your loan-to-value proportion has dropped from 75% to 27%. Looked at like that, paying off your mortgage in the future seems a much less scary prospect.

Still uncomfortable with the idea? Here's the point that most people miss: having an interest-only loan doesn't mean you *can't* repay chunks of the capital if you want to. Yes, fixed-rate deals (to be explained shortly) will have an initial period when you're penalised for overpaying, but after a while (when the fixed-rate period ends or you remortgage) you'll be free to pay off capital at will.

That's truly the best of both worlds. Benefit from the extra monthly cashflow with an interest-only deal, let the cash build up in the bank, then you can decide to use those savings to pay off capital or not – depending on what seems like the best idea at the time. All you're doing is giving yourself more flexibility, because you're not locked into a set repayment schedule.

Making use of equity in your home

Many people get started in property investment by extending their residential mortgage and releasing equity that's built up in their own home. They then use the money to put down a deposit on a property, or even buy it outright.

It's common, but not for everyone: if you've dreamed for years of finally paying off your mortgage completely, you might not appreciate the idea of ramping it up again to buy more property.

Whether you want to bring your own home into play is a completely personal decision for you (and your partner). But if you do, there are a few things to keep in mind.

Firstly, yes, it's possible. Lenders vary, but most won't be fazed if you say you want the money to buy another property. The amount you can borrow will be determined by two things:

1. The value of your home. With residential mortgages, you'll often be able to borrow around 90% of the property's value – which is more relaxed than buy-to-let where (as we'll see in a minute) the maximum "loan-to-value" is usually around 80%.

2. Your income – because residential mortgages are offered as a multiple of your salary. Again, this is different from buy-to-let mortgages where (as we'll see) your income is only a small factor, and the amount they'll lend is based on the rental income the property can generate.

So let's say you have a home worth £500,000, of which you have £100,000 still outstanding on the mortgage. Based on its value, a lender might allow you to borrow up to £450,000 (90% of its value). But they might also cap the amount they'll lend at 5x your income. If you earn a salary of £50,000, that would cap your borrowing at £250,000. So in this case, as your loan is already £100,000, you'd be allowed to borrow an extra £150,000.

The obvious upside of extending the borrowing on your own home is that you can use the cash you release as a deposit on a new property, allowing you to buy even if you don't have any savings to put in. You'll also find that the interest rate you'll pay on a residential mortgage is generally lower than on a buy-to-let loan. The disadvantage is that pretty much all new residential loans are going to be on a capital repayment basis. This means that £100,000 borrowed against your own home might have a lower interest rate than the same amount borrowed against a buy-to-let property, but your monthly repayments might end up being higher because you have no choice but to pay off the capital as well as the interest.

Something else to bear in mind: if you release equity from your home to serve as a deposit, and then use a buy-to-let mortgage to fund the rest of the purchase, the property you're buying is effectively 100% mortgaged. That's fine, but it means you'll need to consider both sets of payments when calculating whether the deal stacks up – and it'll therefore be more challenging to find purchases that will make you a monthly profit.

How much can you borrow?

The amount you can borrow on a buy-to-let property is determined by both its value and the rental income it brings in. Your own circumstances aren't irrelevant, but the lender is far more interested in the property than they are in you:

- They want to be sure of its value because if they need to repossess, they'll sell it to get their money back.

- They want to know its income-generating potential to be sure that the investment will be self-financing (so you can meet your repayments regardless of what else is going on in your financial life).

The maximum loan-to-value (the proportion of a property's value that you can borrow) on a buy-to-let loan at the moment is 85%, but there are very few of those deals around: a more typical level is 75%. So if you want to buy a property for £100,000, you'll need to put down a £25,000 deposit from your own funds and they'll lend you the rest. Of course, you can always borrow lower amounts – and as you get down to 60% loan-to-value and below, the interest rates often decrease.

Lenders use something they call "rental cover" to assess whether the investment is self-financing. Most buy-to-let lenders are regulated by the Bank of England's Prudential Regulation Authority (PRA), who (at the time of writing) insist that the rent must cover at least 125% of the mortgage payment – assuming that the interest rate is at least 5.5%.

(This doesn't apply to certain "specialist" lending such as bridging, commercial or semi-commercial property and holiday lets, nor to *any* lending with a fixed term of five years or longer. You also don't have to worry about any of this if you're re-mortgaging an existing property without increasing the debt, because that also escapes these rules.)

Example time! Let's say you buy a £100,000 property with a mortgage of £75,000. Working from the notional interest rate of

5.5% (*it doesn't matter if your actual interest rate is lower: they'll be making their calculations on the basis that it's 5.5%*), your monthly mortgage payment would be £343.75 (£75,000 multiplied by 0.055, divided by 12 to get the monthly amount). The lender would therefore want the monthly rental income to be at least £429.68 (£343.75 multiplied by 1.25) in order to give you the loan you asked for.

Different lenders vary in their criteria. While the regulations dictate that they need at least 125% rental cover, some lenders will go further and require 135% or 145%. Others will test more stringently in certain circumstances based on your tax position and other liabilities.

The PRA also insists that lenders use tougher criteria to assess mortgage applications from "portfolio landlords" – which they define as someone with four or more mortgaged properties. This means that lenders must take into account income and liabilities across the investor's entire portfolio rather than just look at the proposed new investment in isolation, which means more paperwork to pull together during the application process.

What lenders want to know about you

That was the property. Now let's talk about the other thing that lenders will be looking at: you.

As I've said, for buy-to-let mortgages, lenders won't scrutinise every last KFC receipt like they tend to do for lending on your own home. The property is their main concern, but the number of mortgage options open to you will certainly depend on your personal circumstances.

There are hundreds of buy-to-let products available, and a good broker (a subject we'll come to later) should be able to place you with *something* almost irrespective of your circumstances. However, you'll have a wider selection of the market available to you – which will mean more choice, better rates, higher loan-to-value ratios, and so on – if your broker is able to tick certain boxes for you.

The first box to tick is having a non-property income of at least £25,000 – which can be a joint income if, for example, you and your spouse are buying the property together. While the amount they'll lend is based on rent rather than a multiple of your income, most lenders want to see that you have *some* income so you'll be able to service the debt if the property is empty for a period of time. Different lenders have different "minimum income" requirements, but £25,000 is fairly typical. They specify "non-property income" because, again, if your whole income comes from rents then there's always the possibility that you'll have multiple empty properties and be unable to pay.

This requirement can cause issues for freelancers or contractors, who find it harder to demonstrate their income than an employee who can just show payslips. Lenders typically want to see at least two years of accounts, but again, a good broker can look for exceptions to the rule.

The next box to tick is owning your own residential home. This is less to do with financial security (although it helps) than avoiding fraud: because buy-to-let lending criteria are more relaxed than residential, it's not uncommon for people to get a buy-to-let mortgage on a property they actually want to live in themselves. Having your own home already reduces that risk in the eyes of the lender.

(And let's be clear for a moment: using a buy-to-let loan on a property you want to live in, *or* getting a residential mortgage on a property you intend to let out, are both mortgage fraud and are seriously not a good idea – however many people tell you they've been doing it for years and "the lender doesn't care as long as they get paid every month".)

Another factor lenders will look at is whether you have property experience already – which, of course, doesn't help when you're brand new to property investment.

So if you're starting out with no provable income, no home of your own and no investment properties... it's going to be tough, but not impossible. If you do manage to find a lender who'll accept you, the interest rate they offer you will be less competitive than normal because they need to price in the extra risk, and they might also offer you a lower loan-to-value ratio.

As time goes on and you become an "experienced landlord", it does get easier... until it starts getting harder again, because many lenders will limit the number of properties you can have with them. While in theory you can have as many mortgages as you want, the reality is that some small lenders will reject you if you have more than a certain number of mortgages in total (or they'll restrict the number you can have with them).

A specialist type of personal circumstance is being an expat – a status that makes life particularly tricky when it comes to mortgages, because most lenders want you to be resident in the UK.

More lenders are opening up to lending to expats than has been the case in recent years. Even so, the process can be lengthy, and fees tend to be higher because there's so much more administration involved in verifying what you've told them and ruling out fraud. And as always, criteria vary: some will only lend to expats who are resident in certain countries or who work for recognised global employers, while others will require accounts to be certified by specific firms of accountants. The minimum loan size can also be higher for expats than UK residents, because mortgage companies want to lend a reasonably sized amount to justify the time put into processing the application.

So if you're an expat, getting a mortgage is by no means impossible – but working with a specialist broker is definitely advisable, and healthy reserves of patience are preferable.

Finally, there's the possibility that you'll want to buy a property within a limited company rather than your own name, which is another factor that will reduce the number of options open to you. As a result of less choice, fees and rates will generally be higher – although as buying within companies becomes more popular, competition is increasing and costs are coming down.

Even though the company is the buyer, the lender will make all the same checks on you (as the company director) as they would if you were buying in your own name, and will generally insist on a personal guarantee from you too.

What to look for in a mortgage product

As I'll explain later, I'm pretty insistent about why you should use a broker (a really good broker, at that) to find your mortgage deal for you. But if you're to validate what they come back to you with, it's important to understand the factors affecting the attractiveness of different mortgage products.

The most obvious one is the amount they'll lend you: the loan-to-value. Historically it's been higher, but at the moment 80% is about as high as you can get (with the odd 85% out there), with the majority of products being at 75% and 60%. Of course, there's no rule that says you have to take as much as the product allows: if you only want to borrow 40%, that's fine.

The other big factor is the interest rate. This is a reflection of the risk the lender is taking on, which is a combination of factors around the property, you, and the amount of security they have. As a general rule, interest rates will be higher for 75% loans than 60% because the risk is higher.

The interest rate offered may be fixed or variable. Fixed rates range from two years up to as many as ten; their obvious advantage is that your monthly payment will remain the same for the entire time, so you can have certainty about what your biggest cost will be. Variable rates could just be the lender's "standard variable rate", which they can change whenever they fancy (although usually prompted by changes to the Bank of England base rate), or they could be a "tracker" rate, which moves precisely in line with either the Bank of England rate or the LIBOR rate. Variable rates introduce risk into your business model, but can work in your favour if rates fall: there are some very lucky people out there on "base rate minus 0.5%" trackers who've had years of paying zero interest.

Interest rates, however, are just one component of the cost you end up paying: loans also come with arrangement fees, which can either be a set amount (like £995) or a percentage of the total amount you want to borrow (often from 0.5% to 2%). There are also various valuation fees, account set-up fees and "because we feel like it" fees.

So as you can see, this isn't just a matter of seeing who appears at the top of the "lowest rates" table and giving them a call: you need to first look at each lender's criteria to see who will accept the circumstances surrounding you and the property, then think about how much you want to borrow and how long you want to fix for, *then* start comparing the various combinations of interest rates and fees to see which actually works out the cheapest over the lifetime of the loan.

And so far, I've been assuming that we're looking at a bog-standard buy-to-let house rented out to a single working family.

As soon as you deviate from that, a new world of complication opens up…

Financing "niche" investments

Just as the number of potential lenders reduces as you start to depart from their "ideal" client profile (homeowner, income above £25,000, experienced landlord…), you also start to have fewer options when the property you're buying departs from the norm. Unfortunately, lenders' definition of "the norm" is very narrow – and can exclude relatively common situations.

Two types of properties that lenders don't like are flats above shops, and flats in a block of more than five storeys. The logic makes sense: high-rise flats tend not to be the most desirable, and there can be issues with flats above shops because you can't control which type of business starts operating below you. And yet it's common for swanky (and desirable) new blocks of flats to have six or seven storeys with retail on the ground floor. If you're buying this type of property, it's another reason why having a good broker is invaluable: they should have the relationships to make sure the property is judged on its merits rather than rejected out of hand (a flat in a brand new block of six storeys may not strictly meet criteria, but it's a very different proposition from an ex-council tower block of 20 storeys).

Lenders can also be funny about renting to students, or people who receive housing benefit. This seems like a strange one to me because students can make for very secure tenants (you'll normally have their rent covered by a guarantor), and any tenant could become reliant on housing benefit overnight if they lose their job. But nevertheless, it's something to keep in mind.

And finally, there are multi-lets. Every lender will have a slightly different definition of what they'll lend on: some will allow a certain number of unrelated occupants if they're all on the same tenancy agreement, some will allow separate agreements but insist that bedroom doors don't have key-operated locks, others will go up to a certain number of rooms but not beyond... it's complicated. By the time you get into the realm of licensed HMOs with more than five bedrooms, you're looking at a few specialist lenders only.

Again, it all comes down to the multiplication of factors: if you're a first-time landlord wanting to get into large multi-lets, you'll have few options because most of the specialist lenders want you to demonstrate property experience. If you start out with a simple buy-to-let, you'll find it easier to get accepted by the specialist lenders in future because you'll have experience.

Finding a great broker

You've now seen that getting a mortgage is a whole lot trickier than just choosing the lender with the lowest rate: what *seems* to be the lowest rate may not be by the time you've factored in other fees – and in any case, their criteria might be such that you (or the property you're buying) might not be eligible anyway.

Every lender publishes their rates and criteria online, so there's nothing to stop you from going through all of them and working out the best option for yourself – and indeed, I know people who do exactly this. Personally though, I can think of more enjoyable things to do with my time than comb through the small print of financial documents (clue: almost anything) – and it's also worth bearing in mind that some lenders will only work through an intermediary (i.e. a broker or financial adviser), so you won't have access to the whole market if you're out on your own.

By having a broker on your team, you'll also have someone to sense-check any potential investments before you go too far with them. For example, I recently spotted a property that I thought I might be able to buy quickly with cash then refinance later. I pinged an email to my broker, and ten minutes later she told me that (for a reason I'd never have thought of) it'd be impossible to get lending. None of my time was wasted, and I didn't damage my relationship with the estate agent by making an offer that I'd have needed to withdraw later.

A final advantage of a broker – a really good broker – is that he or she will be in a position to keep your application on track when something weird and unexpected happens. And maybe it's just me, but something weird or unexpected *always* seems to happen at some point during the process.

Take the last two mortgages I applied for: with one the lender freaked out because they somehow got the idea that the vendor was about to go bankrupt (he wasn't), and with the other they thought I owed £29 to British Gas from a year ago and therefore wasn't someone who they wanted to lend money to (I didn't). In both cases, my broker was able to speak to an actual human, explain the facts, and get things back on track.

So for all these reasons, I'd always use a broker.

Not all brokers are as good as mine, but there are a fair few around if you look hard enough. **So what *does* constitute a really good broker?**

- They have access to the whole of the market. A "whole of market" broker will scour every available lender to find you the most suitable product, which of course is exactly what you want. This is why it's a truly terrible idea to walk into your high street bank and speak to the in-house broker there: they'll only be able to offer you products from their own range, which will probably be inferior to other options that they're not allowed to tell you about. Even outside of banks, some independent brokers are "tied" to offer only a limited range, so should be avoided.

- They do the majority of their business in buy-to-let rather than residential. Buy-to-let is a totally different ball game from residential, and someone who only does a couple of buy-to-let cases each month isn't going to have the same depth of experience as someone who does it day-in day-out.

- They aren't just a "processor". Much like solicitors (which we'll come to later), those brokers who work for big national companies often just process what they're given without thinking about it too much – not because they're daft, but because the business model is set up to push through as many transactions as quickly as possible. You want someone who's going to take the time to ask the right questions at the right time.

- They have strong relationships. As I've explained, weird things happen – and when they happen, you want your broker to be able to fire off a quick email to their person on the inside and straighten it out. This is something you'd never be able to do on your own, so for me it's one of the biggest strengths of using a broker.

- They invest in property personally. A fellow investor will understand your priorities better than someone who only deals with investors in the abstract. They'll be able to ask the right questions at the outset to determine your priorities, and match you with a product accordingly, because they've been through the same thought process many times themselves. It makes a huge difference to the quality of advice you get.

You'll notice that I haven't mentioned fees anywhere – and that's because it just isn't as important as everything I've mentioned. Getting the right advice could save you thousands of pounds over the life of a mortgage, so I'm not going to start quibbling over £100 here and there.

When a broker successfully arranges a loan for you, they'll usually be paid a commission by the lender. Some brokers will charge you a fee too, while others won't. My slight preference, oddly, is for brokers who charge me a fee – because it means they have less of an incentive to place me with the lender who pays them the biggest commission, rather than the one that's best for my needs. It's also the case, logically, that if they're getting paid more per transaction, they'll need to do fewer transactions to pay their bills and therefore will give me more time.

That said, from everything I've heard from the experiences of other investors, there seems to be very little correlation between quality and price.

Where do you find a good broker? Recommendations are by far the best way – by which I mean recommendations from investors who operate the same kind of model that you want, rather than from your uncle who's just remortgaged his own home. There's also **unbiased.co.uk** which contains a directory of mortgage brokers (as well as financial advisers and other professions) along with ratings from their past clients.

Quick note: when buying through an estate agent, you'll sometimes be put under pressure to use their in-house broker. Occasionally you might even be told that they'll only put your offer forward if you speak to their broker first. This is because it generates extra income for the branch (at the low end of the market, this can sometimes be more than the fee they'll get for selling the property), and also partially because they're used to having their time wasted with offers from people who it turns out can't get finance.

If you don't want to do so, don't be afraid to say no: they *must* pass on your offer to the vendor whatever the circumstances, and a confident "I have my own broker who I always use" is usually enough to shut the conversation down. Even better, get a broker to arrange a "decision in principle" for you (a quick automated check from a lender that you'll be suitable to borrow once you've found a property) to give the agent confidence that you've got your act together and are ready to proceed.

Flips and auction purchases

Although mortgages are the most common way to finance property investments, there are some situations where they're not an appropriate tool for the job. Two of the most common situations are buying at auction, and "flipping" (also known as "trading" and "buying to sell" – which all refer to buying with the intention of selling for profit as soon as possible, without renting it out first.).

Mortgages aren't suitable for auction purchases because you can't guarantee that they'll be arranged quickly enough. Once the hammer falls you normally have 28 days to complete the purchase – which *can* be enough time to arrange a mortgage, but only if everything goes in your favour. As you can't start the process until after the auction (because you don't know for sure what you'll be buying), it's a very tall order.

One way in which you *can* use a mortgage for auction purposes would be if you were planning to use the equity in your own home to fund the purchase. In this scenario you could go through the whole process of arranging the remortgage of your own home in advance, after which you normally get a window of three to six months before you have to "draw down" the funds. You therefore get the security of knowing that the funds are in place, without having to actually get the cash and start making the repayments until you've secured the property you want. That's going to be a niche situation, but worth mentioning because it's a nice option if it applies to you.

There's a different reason why mortgages aren't suitable for flips: they're meant to be a long-term form of finance, and mortgage lenders don't like you taking their money for just a few months. While it's possible to get a mortgage with no early redemption penalty and just pay the whole lot back (say) six months after you take it out, and it's *also* possible that you'll get away with it a few times, eventually someone will notice and see that you're (in their opinion) abusing what's supposed to be a long-term product. As lenders share information between them, you could end up being blacklisted by multiple lenders – and struggle to get any kind of mortgage in future.

So if mortgages aren't the right tool for the job in these situations, what is? Well, you only have two real choices: cash, or bridging finance.

Cash is self-explanatory, and the great benefit is that it's free apart from the "opportunity cost" of having the funds tied up and not earning a profit elsewhere. For auction purchases that you intend to keep for the long term, you can buy with cash, then remortgage (coming up in the next section) in the future to pull some of your funds back out.

Bridging finance is short-term lending (lasting usually six to 12 months), which carries a higher interest rate than a mortgage but is much quicker to arrange. As a rough rule of thumb, you can normally borrow up to 70% of the property's value.

It's quicker because a bridging lender really doesn't care about you (other than basic checks that you are who you say you are, and haven't been declared bankrupt): their security is the property you're buying. As a result, a bridging loan can be arranged start-to-finish within a week (whereas it can take months for a mortgage to go through).

Another advantage of bridging when it comes to flips and auctions is that they'll lend against properties that would be considered "unmortgageable". Broadly speaking, you can only get a mortgage on properties that could be lived in at the point of taking out the loan: they might not be luxurious, but they need to have a functioning kitchen and bathroom and be structurally sound. Bridging lenders don't care: sure, the value of the property might be reduced if it's a total uninhabitable wreck, but they'll lend against whatever its value is all the same.

You'll be able to see why this is particularly handy for flips (where you might want to buy a wreck, fix it up and sell it on) and auction purchases to either flip or keep (because properties often end up in auction in the first place because there's a problem that renders them unmortgageable).

I said that it carries a higher interest rate than a mortgage, and that interest rate is usually in the range of 0.75%–1.5% per month. On top of that you can add an arrangement fee of 1–2%, a valuation fee, their legal fees, and a grab-bag of other "because we can" fees. (My favourite, which made me laugh semi-hysterically before suddenly getting very sad the first time it was charged to me, being a "repayment administration fee". Yes, they charge you for their effort in receiving their money back at the end.)

Bridging, then, can look expensive by the time you've factored everything in. But if cash and mortgages aren't an option and it allows you to do a deal that's ultimately going to make you a lot of money, is it really expensive? Just factor the costs into your projections and see if it still stacks up. Be aware, though, that you need to be *very* confident that you'll be able to exit the bridge at the end of the term by either refinancing or selling – otherwise they'll crank up the interest rate or could even repossess.

There are a couple of nice tricks you can use with bridging finance too. Firstly, some bridging companies will lend against the property's *value* rather than the purchase price – which means that if you do some amazing negotiation and secure a property for £70,000 when it's genuinely worth £100,000, then the loan will be 70% of £100,000 and you won't have to put any of your own money in (except for fees, refurb costs, etc.) This would never happen with a mortgage, as mortgage loans are always based on the lower of the value or the purchase price.

The other trick comes into play if you have no mortgage (or a very low mortgage) on your own home or another property you own. In this case you could get a bridging loan that takes security against the property you're buying *and* your other property, which again means you can effectively borrow the whole purchase price. You could even borrow enough to cover your refurb fees and costs, too – thus putting none of your own money in. The downside is that your bridging costs would obviously be higher as a result, which would need to be factored into your calculations. And, of course, your home is at risk if the deal goes wrong for some reason.

Remortgaging

Remortgaging is something you might end up doing for any number of reasons. Some of the most common are:

- You want to let out a house that you've lived in yourself up until now. You will need to switch from a residential mortgage to a buy-to-let mortgage.

- You bought a property with cash or bridging, and now you want to move it onto a long-term mortgage to release your cash or get off an expensive bridge onto a cheaper form of finance. (Somewhat confusingly, it's known as "remortgaging" even when you initially bought with cash and are therefore taking out a mortgage for the first time.)

- You've had a mortgage product for a few years and the fixed rate has come to an end. Lower interest rates are now available elsewhere if you switch.

- The value of your property has increased over time (either because of work you've done or just the market moving upwards), meaning you can borrow more money while still staying inside the maximum loan-to-value. This allows you to release funds to invest elsewhere.

You need to use a solicitor for any remortgage transaction, who will take care of the mechanics of adding and removing legal charges and repaying the previous lender (if there is one). I'm often asked how remortgaging actually works in practice, and that's the answer: you'll agree a loan with the new lender, your solicitor will receive the money and use it to pay back the old lender, and any balance left over is deposited in your bank account.

Just as would happen if you were taking out a loan against a property for the first time, in a remortgage scenario the lender will want to conduct a valuation, see the tenancy agreement if there is one, check that any work that's been carried out meets regulations, and so on. But as far as anything involving solicitors and large amounts of money can be, the process is relatively painless.

With the mechanics out of the way, we can now take a more detailed look at each of the situations I outlined earlier.

1. You want to let out a property that you've previously lived in yourself.

At this point it's worth reiterating that YES, you do need to switch from a residential to a buy-to-let mortgage if you're no longer living there, and NO, it's not true that "the lender doesn't care as long as they're getting paid every month". It might be the case that they don't notice right away, but when they do notice (and they're in the habit of checking the electoral roll, for example), bad things will happen. It's a breach of your mortgage terms, and they'd be within their rights to demand immediate repayment in full.

The only exception is if your lender agrees to give "consent to let". This means that you stay on the same mortgage, but they agree that you can let the property out for a period of time – an arrangement that's designed for people who need to move away for work for a while, for example. As is a common theme, the specifics depend on the lender: some won't give consent to let at all, the ones that *will* all allow different periods of time, and some will increase the interest rate you have to pay while others won't. In almost all cases there'll be some kind of admin fee to pay.

If you're remortgaging from residential to buy-to-let (rather than getting consent to let), potential lenders will assess it just like any other buy-to-let loan: they'll conduct a valuation and offer up to a certain loan-to-value, and will also assess the rental valuation and insist that the rental income covers the mortgage by a certain amount (commonly 125%).

There are clearly pitfalls here: as residential mortgages can be offered up to 90% loan-to-value while buy-to-let seldom goes above 80%, you might not have enough equity in your property to switch. Also, if you live in a relatively large or expensive house, you might find that the rent you could achieve wouldn't cover the mortgage payments by 125%.

2. You want to move from cash or bridging onto a mortgage.

This could come about in situations where:

- You bought at auction, and therefore didn't have time to arrange a mortgage.

- You bought a property that needed so much work doing to it that it wasn't mortgageable, and have now fully refurbished it.

- You were able to secure a great price by moving quickly, again not allowing time to arrange a mortgage.

In these situations you might want to refinance straight away (to free up your cash or escape an expensive bridging arrangement), but there's an obstacle to contend with called "the six-month rule".

This is actually a guideline rather than a rule, but it's enforced by the majority of lenders. It states that you must have owned a property for six months before you can apply to remortgage it. What this means is that if you buy a property with cash or bridging for whatever reason, you need to budget for having your cash tied up or your bridging repayments running for at least six months – actually longer, because you can only *apply* after six months of ownership and it might take another month or two for the mortgage to be arranged.

Not all lenders enforce the guideline (especially those termed as "commercial" lenders, who finance HMOs and developments), but most do – so it's always a smart move to have six to eight months in your mind as the minimum period before you can remortgage.

3. You've had a mortgage product for a few years and the fixed rate has come to an end. Lower interest rates are now available elsewhere if you switch.

Mortgage products often come with preferential rates for the first few years, after which they revert to the lender's "standard variable rate" (SVR). For example, you might get a two-year fixed-rate mortgage with a rate of 3.49%, and at the end of the two years it reverts to an SVR of 4.99%.

That means there are two reasons to move away: you'll be able to secure a lower rate by switching to another lender and benefiting from their tempting "introductory" rate for a couple of years, and you'll be able to fix your rate again if you want to. Standard variable rates are (obviously) variable and can change whenever the base rate changes or the lender just feels like it, whereas fixed rates give you certainty over your outgoings during that period.

While it's tempting to just hop from mortgage to mortgage every couple of years to get the best rate, don't forget to factor in fees. Every time you switch there'll be legal fees, valuation fees, an arrangement fee (usually added to the loan balance but still very much a real cost), broker fees and so on. Shaving 1% off your interest rate and saving £50 per month might sound great, but it's not a smart business decision if it costs you £2,000 in fees and you'll need to do it again in a couple of years.

Once again, this is where a good broker will come into their own in terms of advising you of your options and whether it's worth your while switching.

4. The value of your property has increased over time (either because of work you've done or just the market moving upwards), meaning that you can borrow more money while still staying inside the maximum loan-to-value. This allows you to release funds to invest elsewhere.

Many an impressively sized portfolio has been built on this basis over the last 20 years: buy a property with a 75% mortgage, wait for its value to go up, remortgage to 75% of its *new* value and use the cash you've released to buy another property.

This sounds great, and it is – but it's crucial to consider the impact that refinancing will have on your cashflow.

For example, let's say you bought a property for £100,000 with a 75% mortgage and have seen its value rise to £150,000. You can now remortgage to 75% of £150,000, which is £112,500. That means you can repay your original mortgage, repay yourself your deposit of £25,000, and have £12,500 left over to put towards a deposit somewhere else!

Sounds great, but remember that *even though your loan-to-value is still 75%, you're actually borrowing more money.* So with an interest rate of 5%, your (interest-only) monthly payments would originally have been £312.50 and have now increased to £468.75.

If the monthly rent is £900 then that's not necessarily an issue, but what if it's only £700? By the time you've made the higher repayment and met all your other costs, your cashflow could be almost nothing (or less than nothing) – especially in certain tax situations which we'll come to in the "Tax and accounting" section. And if the rent is only £600, you wouldn't be able to refinance in the first place because you wouldn't meet the rental stress test requirements.

This is a really, really (really) important point: remortgaging is great, but you've got to strike a balance between releasing equity and maintaining cashflow. There's absolutely no point borrowing as much as you can to buy loads of properties if you end up barely breaking even or making a (pre- or post-tax) loss: yes you could end up making a capital gain on all your properties if the market is kind to you, but you've put yourself in a very vulnerable position.

In short, it's all about balance. Remortgaging is a powerful tool, so use it responsibly and consider cashflow above everything else.

Chapter 7

Deciding where to buy

A major source of stress for aspiring property investors is coming to a decision about where to focus their efforts – both in terms of location, and what to buy within that location. Even if you're dead set on operating within a half-hour drive of home so that you can easily self-manage your portfolio, that radius is still going to include areas with a whole range of demographics and housing types. And if you're *not* limited to staying near home… well, then "analysis paralysis" can really set in.

It's quite right to put considerable thought into this decision, because – as we saw in Part 1 – different locations and property types are suited to different strategies and outcomes. But don't drive yourself crazy: while it *does* matter, it's important to know when to stop pondering and start investing.

The key is to let go of the idea of finding the absolute best investment area in the country. New investors from analytical backgrounds often want to build some kind of uber-algorithm that feeds in thousands of data points and spits out the #1 investment that's going to explode over the next decade... but I just don't think it's possible, or indeed necessary.

I know for a fact that I'm not that smart, so I spread my bets by investing in multiple locations and types of property – but even that isn't really necessary. Pick any type of property and any location, and there'll be someone making that type of investment work very nicely for them – because success is determined far more by the specifics of the deals you do (buying the right property at the right price, as part of the right strategy for you) than where you do them.

So: don't stress out. But of course, you're not unreasonable to want some better method than throwing a dart at a page of Rightmove results (which is also liable to damage your laptop) – so let's look at some factors to consider when making your decision.

Home or away?

Before going any deeper, let's set out the scope of the decision: are you going to restrict your search to the area around where you live, or are you prepared to go wherever in the UK you perceive the best opportunity to be?

The choice is yours to make: you can be a thoroughly hands-on investor who stands outside lovingly stroking the bricks every day (although beware that tenants may not appreciate it too much), or you can have almost nothing to do with the place once you've bought it.

Indeed, I've come across people at both ends of the spectrum. In my book Beyond the Bricks, I interviewed one investor who only wanted to own properties within 15 minutes of her home so she could whip around all of them in a couple of hours on a Saturday morning to collect the rent in person. At the other end, many of our clients at Property Hub own properties that they've never seen in the flesh (bricks), in towns they've never visited – and they outsource everything to do with acquisition and management. If you view property purely as an investment, there's no reason why you need to restrict yourself to one you can easily visit – in the same way that you wouldn't avoid buying shares in easyJet because you have a fear of flying.

All the same, you don't need to find the absolute best area of the UK in order to be successful. Investing near home not only cuts down on travel, but also makes use of the local knowledge and connections you've naturally built up over time. The immediate streets around your home might not be the most suitable, but I bet you'll find at least one candidate area if your draw a 45-minute radius around where you live. If that's the case, why complicate matters by looking further afield?

One group that gets particularly hung up on whether to go home or away is Londoners. They know that London is in demand and has historically performed well, but they also know that yields are shockingly low and (depending on their budget) they might not be able to afford anything more than a studio flat in an area which nobody could even call "up and coming" with a straight face.

There are perfectly good reasons to favour investing in London, but one of them shouldn't be a fear of the rest of the country. I get all kinds of questions like "Will I still be able to find professional tenants outside London?", and have seen people's eyes visibly twitch when I suggest that Leeds offers good value. So, Important Note For Londoners: the rest of the country really isn't that scary. People still have jobs. They still live in houses. Some of them even have quinoa in their cupboards. If necessary, get on a train and make a research trip to get comfortable with the idea. You don't even need to take your passport.

(And it's OK: I'm allowed to have a friendly poke at Londoners because I am one.)

How to choose a location

If you can make your particular investment strategy work locally, that's great: all else being equal, near is better than far because it'll take less effort for you to develop an in-depth knowledge of the area (which is extremely important – even if you plan to outsource most of the investment process).

But all else is *never* equal, which is why I never advocate staying local by default.

So if you do want to go further afield, where do you even *start* with deciding where to look?

A logical next step from staying local is picking somewhere that's easily accessible by train – because it makes your fact-finding trips easier, and good train links are a tick in the "fundamentals" box too. An investor I interviewed in Beyond The Bricks primarily invests in areas served by the East Coast rail network, because he happens to live along the line and it makes his life a lot easier. When I asked him about the prospects of certain other areas of the UK, he acknowledged that there was probably a strong investment case but he just couldn't be bothered with going there. Rather than looking for the best investments in the entire country, he focuses on the best investments he can make within a certain self-imposed hassle factor.

Another good reason for picking a certain area is that you have family or friends there. This has dual benefits: it's likely to be somewhere you visit occasionally anyway, and you'll have the beginnings of a network there already. These contacts can pay off: I spoke to an investor from Plymouth who bought a fixer-upper near where his family lives in Birmingham, and before he'd even finished refurbishing the property he'd found tenants through work contacts of his relatives. Even if Auntie Jean doesn't happen to know a potential tenant or a good plumber, she will at least be able to speed up your research by giving you her opinion on the different parts of town and where she'd want to live.

You could also choose an area because you know other people who are successfully investing there. "Coat-tail investing" is a recognised investment strategy when it comes to the stock market, and there's no reason not to follow it in property too: if you know they're getting good results, why re-invent the wheel? There are no bonus points for originality... and if you're friendly with them, you can get their opinions on where to invest and maybe even tap into their local network. I'm only mildly embarrassed to admit that I bought two units in a building in Nottingham purely by copying (with permission) a friend: his research showed that it had particularly strong prospects and I agreed, so why not?

Finally, of course, you could pick an area where none of the above apply but you see a particularly strong investment case – perhaps based on improvements that are planned for the future, demographic changes that you've recognised, or anything else. I'm happy to admit that I'm not that smart, which is why I've listed all the other reasons first – but if you can go against the herd and get it right, you'll deservedly get the very best returns.

Where not to invest

I've said that you don't need to concern yourself with finding the absolute best investment location, but you definitely want to steer clear of areas that *won't* work well. So how can you identify them and stay away?

The best investment areas are underpinned by solid fundamentals: jobs, schools, shops, leisure facilities and transport links. This shouldn't come as a massive surprise, because they're the same factors that you're likely to use when deciding where to live – and "people wanting to live there" is a rather critical concern when assessing a buy-to-let investment.

Areas that don't work are therefore locations with an absence of these fundamentals.

… Which rules out rural locations. Cottages in tiny villages might make for brilliant holiday lets, but for mainstream buy-to-let there just won't be enough demand to put an upward pressure on rents (the population is low, and most people who move there will want to buy).

Also ruled out, for me at least, are areas that lack employment opportunities and don't have good transport links to other centres of employment. A classic example of this is Haverhill in Cambridgeshire: it's only 20 miles from Cambridge but doesn't have its own station, which means it's difficult to travel to nearby towns with good jobs. As a result, property prices are held down compared to the rest of the region, and there's a shortage of professional tenants. Some investors operate very successfully there by targeting the LHA market, but it's not for me – both because of the hassle-factor and the fact that capital growth is unlikely.

So, unless it's part of a deliberate strategy, avoid areas without fundamentals. That doesn't mean you should just plonk your cash anywhere with a few shops, transport links and a gym though: some areas have an abundance of fundamentals yet still make for poor investment locations. Why? Because of a "prestige" factor that makes them relatively expensive places to buy. Places like Chester, Oxford and London fall into this category.

Of course, "expensive" doesn't necessarily mean "poor ROI" if the rents are equally high, but it's generally the case that in areas with very expensive housing, the rents aren't increased by an equivalent amount to make investments stack up. If you bought a house for £500,000, you'd need to rent it out for £2,900 per month to get a 7% yield, which in most cases just isn't going to happen – whereas a £250,000 house renting for £1,450 (achieving the same yield) is easily possible.

When I talk about avoiding certain types of area, I only mean to give general guidelines. Property investment *can* work anywhere, and some people do extremely well in the types of area I've warned you about above. If you know exactly what you're doing, go for it. If you're a beginner, I'm just trying to steer you towards the locations where you'll get the easiest ride.

Getting into more detail

Once you've finally stopped agonising and picked an area to focus on, decisions still need to be made: there's quite a gap between "Manchester is the place for me!" and "Right, I'm off to look at properties!" Which part of Manchester? Where in that area? What type of property in that area? Those are questions you'll want to answer to some extent before you go out shopping.

In every town or city I've researched, no matter how small, I've found a range of areas with different characteristics. Even if you pick somewhere relatively tiny like St Helens (with a population of just over 100,000), there will be parts that are cheaper and more expensive, more and less desirable, geared towards different types of tenants, and so on.

The process I use to better understand the range of opportunities within a town progresses from "embarrassingly vague" to "unbearably specific".

I'll usually start with something as basic as Googling a phrase like "areas in [town]". Somewhere on the first page or two – beyond the Wikipedia and local council links (which can be useful in their own right) – there will normally be some kind of message board thread discussing the pros and cons of different parts of town.

While any single post should be taken with a barrel of salt (and there are usually completely contradictory opinions of the same area within the same thread), over time you'll start to see patterns emerge. Which are the areas (or postcodes) where people always say "avoid"? Which are recommended to people with young families? It sounds simplistic, but as you start learning about these different areas and looking them up on a map, you'll start to develop a surprisingly accurate picture of the general geography of an area.

From this, you can draw up a shortlist of a few areas to look at in more detail. Your shortlist will depend on your strategy. If you're looking for dirt-cheap properties that are likely to yield well, the areas that people say "avoid" might be the first you want to explore. If flipping is your strategy, you need an area with high buyer demand – so you'll be looking for places that families or young couples want to move to. A niche strategy like students or HMOs might take you in a different direction again – with proximity to universities/colleges and transport links respectively being the factors to look for.

The next step for me is always to establish a rough idea of price norms in each area of interest. The quickest (and least accurate) way of doing this is to use a site called **home.co.uk**. Head over there, select "Prices & Rents" and search for the first part of the postcode, such as LS10, M27 or BS3 (the "House Prices" button should be checked). On the results page, look for the link called "Selling prices since 1995". This will show you a variety of reports (broken down by property type, number of bedrooms, etc.) relating to prices now and over time. Now you can see how much, for example, the average three-bedroom property in this postcode will set you back.

You can then repeat the search by going back to the homepage and looking at "Market Rents" reports to get a feel for the kind of rents that are achievable, too. It's exceptionally rough and ready, but by combining the two reports you'll get some idea of where prices are beyond your reach, where rents appear to be reasonably high compared to prices, and so on.

To get meaningful results using **home.co.uk**, your area of interest needs to map with some accuracy to the first part of a postcode. This works brilliantly in some towns, but in others the postcode areas are too large to be of any use. If that's the case, you can skip ahead to the next step: this step was only to give you a rough idea, and the next one gives you much better data anyway.

For a deeper dive, it's time to roll up your sleeves and do a bit of manual Rightmove browsing. (Zoopla works perfectly well too – I just choose to use Rightmove.) Using a full postcode within an area of interest, search for properties for sale within 1/4 mile of that postcode (opening it up to 1/2 mile if you don't get many results). Go straight over to "map view" and start hovering your mouse over each of the pins representing a property for sale, looking out for patterns that emerge.

(To find a full postcode in an area you're interested in, the easiest way is to just Google a shop you can see on the map – its postcode normally comes up in the search result.)

Again this is more of an "art" than "science" approach, but by exploring the map you'll quickly be able to build up a general idea of how much properties cost in a given area – like a range of £100,000 to £130,000 for a three-bedroom house. You'll also start to get a feel for "micro-location": you'll notice undrawn boundaries where a "good" area ends and a "bad" area starts, just by looking at changes in house prices and the type of housing on offer. You'd never have achieved this level of detail from a postcode or a message board thread, but it emerges quickly as you browse around – especially as you get used to doing it.

Then, the natural next step is to repeat the process of browsing the map for properties to rent, to get a feel for how rents vary across the area. By putting these two pieces of information together, you can calculate *very* rough gross yields for different parts of town: multiply what seems to be the average monthly rent by 12, then divide it by what seems to be the average purchase price.

When I perform this process, I inevitably start to get a lot more geeky at some point – finding out lots more about each area while also pinning down the exact prices and rents. For now, though, this is enough: you should have a shortlist of areas that look appropriate to your strategy, are within your price range, and where yields seem to be acceptable.

Of course, there's still further to go before you buy – you need to get from a general area like "Headingley", "Parr" or "Bow" down to the specific streets that you would and wouldn't buy on – but now we're getting into the territory of assessing actual deals, which we'll be covering in the next chapter.

Now that you're more comfortable with identifying areas you'd consider investing in, you're probably starting to think "OK, great… so how do I FIND opportunities in these areas?". That's what we'll get onto next. But first, a few notes:

- I bet you my highest-yielding property that at some point during reading this book the thought "Hmm, should I be looking at houses or flats?" will have popped into your head. In my opinion, it doesn't much matter and I own both. The lack of control you get with blocks of flats is annoying sometimes, but so are all the issues you have to deal with (and pay for) with houses that are taken care of for you with flats. If you have a strong preference for one or the other, that's fine: I won't try to persuade you otherwise. But if you're not religious about these things, just continue to consider both for now.

- This whole research process is, of course, assuming you *have* to figure it all out for yourself. If there's someone you can ask about a particular area (a local letting agent would be good, but even your cousin who's lived there for 20 years would be helpful), that's always going to save time and give you more reliable data.

- If you can, this would be a great point to actually visit the area and test your assumptions about it: you'll build your confidence by putting your new knowledge to the test, and you can also start building up that critical street-by-street knowledge. Over time, you'll find that your research is so well-honed that you're seldom surprised by what you *do* find when you visit, but that probably won't be the case with your first few investments.

Chapter 8

Finding deals

Having pinpointed where you want to buy, now it's a case of finding properties you *can* buy.

If you're happy with an average deal, it's not difficult: go on Rightmove, find something that looks like it meets your criteria and offer 5–10% below the asking price. You'll be the proud owner of a new property before you know it.

It might seem like I'm looking down on this approach, but I'm not at all. Yes, you'll do better if you dig deeper and put more effort into finding great deals, but your strategy might not require it. That's why Part 1 was there: once you've set your goals and your strategy, you can decide how much effort it's worth putting in to dig through the "average" deals in order to find the "good" or the (very rare) "great".

So in this chapter we'll run through some of the main routes to finding property to buy, roughly in ascending order of how time-consuming they are. You can then decide which approach best suits the amount of time you've got to invest – as well as how much effort you *need* to put in for your strategy to work.

Sourcing companies

Sourcing companies, as the name suggests, specialise in sourcing properties (usually off-market opportunities they find through direct advertising or via their network) and passing them on to investors – for a fee, naturally. They're (potentially) a great option for time-strapped investors: they'll send opportunities through, you pick one, job done. There are companies that specialise in all sorts of different types of investment – from off-plan to new-builds to HMOs. There are some that will even source shabby houses and renovate them for you once you've purchased.

Why only *potentially* a great option? Because the quality of opportunities presented by sourcing companies differs so wildly: some are excellent, but I'm signed up to a lot of sourcers' mailing lists and often see exactly the same over-priced property being touted by multiple companies in succession. They'll always say it's wonderful and massage the figures to make it seem more attractive than it is, so the onus is on you to investigate their claims and decide for yourself.

As a result, using a sourcing company will save you a lot of research and travel time, but you'll still want to set aside plenty of time to assess and validate what they send your way. They'll always claim that the property is available "below market value" (something we'll be investigating later), and they'll tell you what sort of rental income can be achieved from it. Depending on the company, those figures can be realistic, optimistic, or downright delusional. In the next chapter you'll learn how to compare their analysis to your own.

Of course, sourcing companies charge a fee – which can be anything from about £1,000 for a small-scale operator who just does a bit of sourcing on the side, to five figures for companies who'll also manage renovation or conversion projects for you. Rather than worrying about what's "fair" or the "right price" to pay, I have a simple test: add their fee to the purchase price of the property. If it still stacks up as a good deal and you couldn't find the opportunity yourself (or at least, couldn't do so without investing an amount of your own time which you value at more than the fee), what does it matter? If someone could save me £10,000, I'd happily pay them £5,000 – even if that included a whacking great profit margin for them.

Estate agents

In case you hadn't noticed, estate agents aren't universally loved and respected. Nevertheless, there's no denying that they see a heck of a lot of properties, and they'll (collectively) represent the majority of the stock for sale in any given area. It would be a mistake to write them off as a source of deals because you object to their branded cars or habit of referring to everything as a "unique opportunity".

The ideal scenario is to become bezzie mates with an estate agent so they'll give you the nod on red-hot opportunities before they hit the open market – because for all their faults, they'll know what's coming up for sale way before anyone else. Realistically though, however charming and good looking you are, this isn't going to happen right away. Speak to any agent and they'll tell you that they're inundated with calls from people who describe themselves as "investors" who are "cash buyers" and can "move fast" and all the rest of it, who turn out to be nothing of the sort. Even if you *are* the real deal, they've already heard so much nonsense from other people that they're totally immune to your claims.

Don't get me wrong: over time it absolutely is possible to build up relationships where you get preferential treatment. After all, what an agent really wants is to be able to shift their stock quickly and easily so they can move on to the next one and hit their monthly targets. If they know an investor who can be relied upon to buy lots of properties and not mess them around, that investor will always get the call first.

But talk is cheap, and particularly so in property – so it's your actions that will build your relationships over time. And until you've achieved speed-dial status, I've got four simple rules for getting the best out of your local agents.

1. Useless agents are your best friends

There are all sorts of estate agents, from big national chains down to solo operators who don't even have an office. The corporates normally do at least a semi-respectable job of marketing properties, but the quality of some smaller agents' efforts is truly shocking.

Which is great news for you! If they're failing to market a property effectively, that means fewer people are going to see it and the vendor is potentially going to be grateful for your (low) offer because barely anyone has been through the door.

A good first filter for poor marketing is finding properties that aren't on the online portals like Rightmove and Zoopla. Failing to put properties online is inexcusable, given that it's where 97% of buyers start their search. But it happens – and because many investors will only ever search online, your competition has already reduced to a fraction of what it would have been. So drive around your target area looking for "for sale" boards, note down the addresses, then cross-reference them against the portals. You can also check the local paper, which will normally have a property supplement on a specific day of the week where small ads will run.

With properties that *have* made it to the portals, I always get excited when I see ones with either just a sole external photo or internal photos that make it look like an absolute tip. Marketing like this is going to put off almost all potential owner-occupiers, and a good number of lazier investors too – so these are the first ones I call up about.

Also look out for properties listed with "online agents". As these agents are basically "listing only" services for a set fee, they're not going to be pushing their listings very hard – and often the vendors themselves will be doing the viewings. This is an opportunity to get in there and make your case to the vendor directly, cutting the agent out of the loop.

2. Follow up

Around 30% of properties that are "sold subject to contract" will fall through and end up back on the market again (which is why agents value buyers who don't mess them around so highly).

Sales that have fallen through are brilliant opportunities, because by that point the vendor is emotionally invested in moving (and has maybe even committed to another purchase), and will be far more open to a low offer than they would have been a couple of months previously. So if you've viewed a property and been outbid (or enquired about a property that was already under offer by the time you called), follow up.

By "follow up", I don't mean "send an email at some unspecified future point": I mean "call the agent every week until they tell you that it's exchanged and the deal is going ahead". You might think that agents keep lists of people who've expressed an interest in a property – so that they have something to fall back on for the one-in-three times that a deal falls through. But this happens approximately 0% of the time. In order to swoop in you need to be bugging the agent through the weeks when they're getting twitchy about the sale not happening, and phone them at the exact point that they're just about to re-list it.

You'll feel like an idiot or a stalker at first, but you'll be amazed at how often it gets results – and even if it doesn't work, you're still cementing yourself in the agent's mind as a serious investor who's a cut above all the dreamers they normally have wasting their time.

3. Be nice

Never forget that agents are working for the vendor rather than you, but that's no reason not to have an enjoyable working relationship. It's no secret that people are more willing to help people they like, so it's a smart business move to be a pleasant person to deal with. It also makes the whole process a lot more fun than approaching everything as a battle that needs to be won.

One easy thing you can do to make an agent's life easier is give clear and helpful feedback on what you think about properties you've viewed. Agents can feel resentful that they've taken the time to drive to a property, wait for you and walk you all around it… only for you to vanish and fail to return their calls asking for feedback. They need to be able to tell the vendor about the reactions they're getting, so help them out a bit: pro-actively tell them why you're not interested, without being unnecessarily scathing. Simply saying "It needs more work than I expected" or "The third bedroom is too small for it to work for me" will give them something to work with – and also gives them an opportunity to hint that a lower offer would still be welcomed, if that's the case.

4. Do what you say you'll do at all costs

Relationships with agents take a lot of time to build, but can be destroyed with just one action. It's not hard to see why: they promise their client that they've found a buyer who can pay a certain amount or complete within a certain timescale, and it puts them in a very awkward position if that turns out not to be the case.

It's worth keeping this in mind and taking a long-term approach to the relationship, even if it costs you money in the short term. Did you say you'd complete in 30 days but are now having trouble with your mortgage application? It might be worth seeing if the numbers still add up if you use bridging finance to complete, and worry about the mortgage later. Have you un-covered something at the last minute that's going to cost you £1,000 to put right? Consider taking it on the chin rather than forcing the agent to tell their client that you're lowering your offer at the eleventh hour.

It won't always make sense to take a financial hit to protect the relationship, but the point is that being a "safe bet" is the attrib-ute that will eventually lead to you getting the nod on those rare amazing deals that come along. Be wary about over-promising, and make sure you always deliver.

Auctions

Rob's Golden Rule Of Auctions #1: There's always a reason why a property has ended up at auction instead of going through the normal selling channels. Before you bid, you need to find out what that reason is.

It could be because the vendor is in a rush and needs the certainty of the sale once the hammer falls, which is fine. It could be because it's in disastrous internal condition and there's no point having an estate agent attempt to market it to ordinary "retail" buyers, which is also fine.

But it could be because it has a very short lease, or sitting tenants on a protected tenancy, or major structural problems, or is subject to a strange covenant that restricts its use. Any of these may or may not be fine, depending on your area of expertise and appetite for risk, but *you need to know* – so you can factor the cost of remedial action into your maximum bid. If you haven't worked out what the problem is, you can't bid effectively.

Rob's Golden Rule Of Auctions #2: Just because it's in an auction doesn't make it a bargain.

You can blame Homes Under The Hammer for this one. Thanks to this type of TV show, there's a general public opinion that auctions are the place to go to pick up a bargain property. Which, as the number of attendees increases, naturally raises demand and means that isn't necessarily the case.

In fact, there's a small sub-set of investors who pick up shabby properties that have been poorly marketed by estate agents (where demand is low), then stick them straight into auction (where demand is high) without doing anything to them at all.

Their profit margin comes from the fact that amateur auction buyers will unwittingly bid more than they'd have paid by just buying through an estate agent – because they *assume* that because it's in auction and looks like a bit of a wreck it must be a bargain.

For disciplined and serious investors, this is the major problem with auctions: you can set yourself a very sensible maximum bid based on the property's realistic value, then get outbid by amateurs who've either got their sums wrong or just want "a project" and haven't budgeted in a profit margin or the cost of their own time.

For this reason (as you're probably picking up), I'm not a fan of buying at auction. It's frustrating to have to thoroughly research multiple properties – and you must be thorough, because if you make the winning bid, you've bought it and there's no backing out – then not end up being able to buy any of them.

But I can't deny that the simplicity of the sale being guaranteed when the hammer falls (rather than commencing months of legal nonsense) is appealing, and it works well for a lot of people – so let's take a quick look at the defining features of an auction purchase.

Auction houses will publish their catalogue for upcoming auctions about a month in advance, and there will normally be a few set times where "block viewings" will take place for each property: the auctioneer will open up and hang around for an hour, and anyone who's interested can just show up without an appointment. Each property will also have a "legal pack" – the contents of which vary, but will usually include documents like local searches, the title plan, and so on. Legal packs need to be available before the day of the auction, but won't always be in place by the time the property appears in the catalogue. Depending on the auctioneer, there will sometimes be a service where you register your interest and they'll email you whenever the legal pack is updated.

Ideally, before bidding, you'll want to physically inspect the property and get your solicitor to look over the legal pack. This is where things can get tricky: you don't want to pay a solicitor a fortune to look at a property you might not be able to buy, and they won't be willing to look at a bunch of potential purchases just as a favour. As you build up a relationship and they realise that you can send a fair bit of work their way, you might be able to persuade them to give the legals a quick glance for free or a small fee.

Ideally again, you'd get a full survey undertaken on each property you're interested in (we'll discuss surveys in more detail later). In reality though, it's just far too expensive to incur that kind of cost when you don't have any certainty that you can get it for the right price. This is a big reason why I don't recommend auctions to people without building skills or contacts: as an amateur it's very hard to know whether just a cosmetic refurbishment is needed or if there's something serious going on. If you can persuade a builder to come along to the block viewing with you to give an opinion and roughly cost up the work involved, that's a huge plus.

Then, of course, you need to determine your maximum bid – which is no different from assessing any other deal, and will be the subject of the next chapter. By now you should know what's wrong with the property (remember: there will always be something), and factor that into your bid. Each property will have a "guide price", which you can completely ignore: sometimes guides are set deliberately low to encourage people to view the property and kick off the bidding, and in any case they shouldn't have any bearing on how much it makes sense for *you* to be paying. There will sometimes also be a "reserve price" (which won't be published), meaning that if the maximum bid falls below that price, the sale won't happen.

Armed with your maximum bid, you turn up on the day (or participate over the phone, or sometimes online) and **don't exceed it**. If you're prone to getting carried away, take a friend who can be trusted to pin your arms to your sides and march you out of the room once your maximum has been reached. Everyone thinks that they're completely rational, but auctioneers are professionals at creating a charged environment – and, psychologically, once you've invested time and possibly money in researching a property, you're highly motivated to suspend your better judgement and try to make it work.

And as I've said, once the hammer falls, you're legally bound to buy the property – no backing out, at least not without huge expense. You'll be expected to pay the deposit (normally 10%)

plus the auctioneer's fee in person, there and then, with the balance normally due (depending on the exact terms of the auction) 28 days later.

All in all, auctions are something of a double-edged sword: compared to the normal conveyancing process it's wonderful to have the certainty of the sale immediately and the whole thing wrapped up inside a month, but it also forces you to make a decision with very limited information and no chance of backing out if you make a mistake.

There is, however, a way of getting the best of both worlds that I'm quite a fan of: buying *after* auction.

There can be any number of reasons why a property didn't sell at auction – from the ones you might expect (like some major, obvious problem that means nobody will touch it with a barge-pole), down to the reserve price being set too high, to random factors like a lack of viewings because of problems getting access to the property, or a low turnout at the auction that evening because of a major football match (seriously).

Vendors tend to be open to offers after auction, because they're worried: they put it into the auction to have the certainty of a sale, thousands of people saw it in the catalogue, and nobody wants it. As a result, not always but often, they'll be open to low offers that they never would have entertained beforehand. In short, the dynamics have shifted: rather than being just one of hundreds of potential bidders, you're suddenly in the driving seat.

Yes, you'll miss out on some opportunities that *do* sell in the room for less than you would have been willing to pay, but (in my opinion) checking out the unsold lots from auctions can offer a better return on your time: you know that you're in with a reasonable chance of being able to buy everything you're looking at, and there's no risk of getting carried away and exceeding your maximum bid.

Direct to vendor

While the majority of properties being sold end up with an agent or in an auction, not all do. Some people need to sell *right now* and can't wait for the property to be marketed, or don't like the idea of having people walking through their house on viewings for weeks on end, or don't want the neighbours to know they're selling, or have any number of other reasons for wanting to sell "outside the system". There are also people who'd normally put their property on with an agent, but would be happy to have a quick sale and not go through the whole painful process if you can get to them at the right time.

Buying a property in this way – without it being marketed by a third party – is known as going "direct to vendor". It's undoubtedly the most effort out of all the methods we've looked at, but it can also be where the best deals are found.

How do you get in front of the vendor in the first place? Some of the typical approaches include:

- Putting "we'll buy your house for cash" adverts through letterboxes

- Advertising in the local paper

- Putting up small ads in shops

- Advertising on billboards

- Driving around in a branded car

Or ideally, all of the above, repeatedly. Going direct to vendor is a numbers game: only a tiny fraction of the people in any given area will be in a position of needing to sell their house quickly at any given time, and those people are unlikely to even notice your advertising the first time they see it. The trick is to stay visible through all kinds of different channels over time. The fifth time someone gets your leaflet through your door (after already seeing your car parked on the next street and your billboard by the bus stop), the timing might be exactly right, and they'll give you a call.

I won't go into endless detail about how to advertise to vendors, because it's so time-consuming it's just not going to be a viable option for the vast majority of readers. Done properly, advertising and following up on leads is a full-time job – and for most of us, it's more time-efficient to pay a fee to sourcers who've gone direct to vendor to dig up these opportunities in the first place.

Chapter 9

Assessing a deal

Through a combination of one or more of the methods we've run through, you should be well on your way to having a healthy pipeline of potential deals crossing your desk. The next step, of course, is to analyse those deals: which ones fit your strategy and are worth offering on, and what price should your offer be?

My view is that any given property has two prices: its objective market value, and the price that it makes sense for you to pay in order to meet your objectives. **You don't want to pay anything higher than the lower of these two prices:** you don't want to buy a property that's objectively overpriced, but you also don't want to buy a property that's priced fairly if it won't give you the return you need.

In this chapter we'll look at determining how much a property is worth, and what it's worth for *your* purposes in both buy-to-let and buy-to-sell scenarios. We'll also look at assessing a property's rental demand and rental value.

Before we can get into any discussion of market value though, we need to straighten out one of the property industry's most innocuous-sounding yet misunderstood and misused concepts: that of buying *below market value.*

Does "BMV" exist?

One of the most seductive and misunderstood concepts in property investment is the notion of buying below market value, or BMV. If you look on any property forum, one in three posts will be someone asking where they can find BMV property. Another one in three is someone offering a "BMV opportunity". And a good proportion of the final third contain warnings about some company or other ripping someone off over a BMV opportunity.

Given that it's being talked about so much, agreement on exactly *what* constitutes BMV is surprisingly difficult to pin down. Taking its strictest definition, some people will tell you that it's a contradiction in terms: the market value is the price agreed between a willing seller and a willing buyer, so whatever price you pay *is* by definition the market value.

That may be literally true, but I don't think it's very helpful. When most people say "BMV" they mean "buying at a better price than might have been possible under other circumstances". By that definition it's very much achievable – and desirable.

To understand why it's possible, we can contrast the selling of properties with the selling of shares. If you want to buy a share in a company, there's one quoted price – which has been arrived at by weighing up all the people who want to buy and all those who have shares to sell. Everyone knows what the quoted price is, and there's absolutely no chance of being able to buy the share for less than that. We can argue endlessly about what the price *should* be and conclude that the price that's being offered is either cheap or expensive, but there's no way you can buy a share for less than the price actually *is* right now. It's also not necessary to consider who the seller of the share is: you'll be able to buy it for the same price regardless of whether they desperately need to offload it today to avoid bankruptcy or have come to a cool and rational decision to sell today purely out of choice.

In property, none of this is true. If there are two absolutely identical houses next door to each other, it's not hard to imagine situations in which they could each sell for a totally different price:

- The vendor of one house is in a real rush to move. They're willing to slash the price for anyone who can buy in cash within 30 days, because taking a hit on the price is worth it for them to have the certainty of being able to move on.

- One house is on the market with an agency that has a fleet of branded Minis and besuited salespeople who take ten viewers through the house every day. The other is listed with a discount agent who's forgotten to put a board up, and listed it on Rightmove with no photos and the wrong number of bedrooms in the description.

• Three families have fallen in love with the two houses. One of them moves first and makes a straightforward cash offer for property #1, which is accepted. That leaves the two other families to fight it out over the second house, and over the period of a week they desperately keep attempting to outbid each other until the winner secures the property for far more than the original asking price.

As you can see from these examples (and many more you can probably think of), the reason for being able to buy one house more cheaply than the other can be more to do with the circumstances surrounding the sale than the property itself. But that isn't necessarily the case: the condition of a property can be a factor too.

You might expect that a property in need of a £10,000 refurb would sell for £10,000 less than an otherwise identical property that's already in prime condition. That, however, is assuming that buyers are completely rational and make all decisions based on the financials – which isn't the case among owner-occupiers and amateur investors.

If only owner-occupiers were looking around the two properties, I'd expect the one in prime condition to sell for *more* than £10,000 above the one that needed the work. Many prospective buyers would discount the "fixer-upper" out of hand, because they want somewhere that's ready to move into. Others would wrongly estimate the works as costing more than £10,000. And as more people are in the market for the immaculate property next door, a bidding war can be sparked – with people getting emotionally attached to the property and willing to pay more than it's worth.

Does that mean you can snap up any property that needs work at a bargain price? No, because in reality there will always be people looking for "a project", as well as investors actively seeking out properties that need some TLC. But sometimes, the different factors will align in your favour: if you get a mess of a property that's being poorly marketed, or where the owner is desperate to sell and knows they have a limited target market, then a BMV opportunity can be created.

What BMV isn't

So buying BMV is possible. But to know whether you're *actually* buying below market value, you need to know the market value. This is where a lot of investors come unstuck: they equate "cheap" with "BMV" – and they aren't the same thing at all.

Take a pair of two-bedroom flats on adjacent streets, in the same condition, and with the same internal area. Leaving aside any people-factors why the owner of one might be willing to sell for less than its market value, why might the *actual* market value of one be lower than the other?

- There's a railway line at the bottom of the garden and it shakes every time the 11:27 from Edinburgh goes past.

- There are nightmare neighbours on one side who are always throwing rubbish into the garden and shouting abuse, making it an unpleasant place to live.

- The lease has just 50 years remaining on it, which can be extended but only at a cost.

- There's a major works bill looming for cyclical repairs to the roof, which will be taking place in a year.

- It's fractionally outside the catchment area of a very popular school, and the other flat is just inside.

If one of these situations were true and you hadn't considered it, you might come to the conclusion that one of the flats was being sold below market value. In fact, its *true* market value is lower.

That's why, although I firmly believe that BMV does exist as a concept, it's in your interests to have a healthy scepticism towards whether any given deal is genuinely below market value. The thing to remember is that nobody sells a property at a bargain price because they're feeling generous: there will always be a reason, and it's your job to find out what that reason is.

If you discover a problem with a property, that doesn't necessarily mean you should steer clear of buying it – just that you shouldn't be under any illusions about its true value. For example, say that the value of a property is £20,000 lower than otherwise identical properties because of a short lease. If you know that and you're up for the task of extending it, no problem – you might be able to offer £40,000 lower and secure the deal, because most other people are put off when they find out what the situation is.

How to assess market value

When surveyors conduct a valuation on behalf of a mortgage lender, they compare the property to others that have sold recently. The idea is that if an identical property across the road sold for £175,000 a few months ago, that must (in the absence of any other evidence) be the market value.

They'll take into account the condition of the property and reduce or increase its value accordingly, and they might apply a percentage increase if they're confident that the local market has picked up in the intervening months, but it all starts with these "comparables".

So when you're assessing a deal, it makes sense for you to calculate market value in exactly the same way: using **similar** properties, that are very **nearby**, and have **sold** recently. It's no good if they're a mile away or twice the size, and you can't tell anything from a property that sold two years ago or is still on the market and just has an "asking price" (which might be totally disconnected from reality).

Imagine a scenario where you've had a call from your friendly neighbourhood estate agent, who says they've got a gem of a property for you. It's worth £175,000, but the vendor is in a hurry so they've listed it at £160,000 and an offer above £150,000 would probably seal the deal. How do you put to the test their claim that it's worth £175,000? Given a postcode and a set of photos (and ideally, but not necessarily at this stage, an in-person viewing), here's what I'd do:

Step 1: Completely forget everything the agent has said. Pretend that you've been set the task of determining how much the property is worth without even knowing what the asking price is.

Step 2: Fire up Rightmove, and head over to the "Sold house prices" section. The information is pulled from the official Land Registry data, but Rightmove is able to supplement it with extra historical information from its own database. (Zoopla does the same, but I just happen to prefer Rightmove.)

Enter the postcode of the property in question, select a search radius of 1/4 mile (increase it to 1/2 mile if you don't get many results), and select "freehold" or "leasehold" as appropriate to filter out properties that wouldn't be a good match.

Then, unless you can write some kind of fancy algorithm to process the results for you, it's time to scan down the list and see what's what. Annoyingly, there's no way to filter by the number of bedrooms (one of the biggest variables affecting the price), so you just have to go down the list and look for properties with the same number of bedrooms as the property you're interested in. Even more annoyingly, it sometimes doesn't give the number of bedrooms at all – which means you need to exclude that property completely.

The genius of Rightmove is that if the property has been listed on the portal at any point in the past, it will pull through the photos (and sometimes floor plans) that went with the original listing. This allows you to see what the internal condition was like, and try to piece together information to determine how similar its size and layout is to the property you've been offered.

There's no great art to this, but after looking at as many results as you can, you can get a feel for the range of what similar properties were sold for. It might be that those in ordinary condition went for £160,000, those that had been extended or had a big garden went up to £180,000, and perhaps there were some wrecks down towards £140,000. There will usually be some strange outliers too, which sold at a particularly high or low price for no obvious reason.

Although this approach is imprecise and not at all scientific, it can get you closer than you might think – certainly close enough to run some very rough numbers and decide whether it's worth viewing. It doesn't come close to the accuracy you'll be capable of when you know the streets of the area like the back of your hand, but it's good enough for now.

The only real challenge with this method is situations where there just haven't been many comparable sales recently. If this is the case, you can slightly relax your criteria – by looking further back in time, or broadening the area, or looking at different numbers of bedrooms and raising/lowering the price accordingly – as long as you're aware that your rough guess is going to be even rougher as a result. And even though asking prices count for little, I can never resist the temptation to look at the prices of properties on the market right now – just as another data point.

Another tool you can use in your analysis, if you're willing to spend a bit of cash, is a valuation report from Hometrack (**hometrack.com**). It costs £19.95, and is basically an automated version of the process I've just described. Many of the big lenders use it as part of their own research process, so using it can increase your level of confidence.

You can also call local agents and ask them if they've recently sold any properties similar to the one you're looking at: any sales within the last couple of months might not have filtered through to the Land Registry database yet. I'm told that agents are even more willing to talk if you tell them you're a surveyor calling to research a valuation you've been asked to do for a client, but that's a deception too far for me – even though I'm the sort of person who pretends not to speak English when approached on the street by someone with a clipboard.

If the property you're looking at needs work, then of course the cost of the works should be deducted from a comparable property in perfect condition. If I knew the cost of the works I'd deduct them from the "mint condition" price, then deduct another 10% as a contingency, then deduct a further 20% to serve as my reward for putting in the time and effort of refurbishing. In fact, I rarely know the actual cost of the works because I don't have any expertise myself, and I'm not active enough in one geographic area that I can drag a builder out to everything I want to view. At the early stages then, I tend to just make a very pessimistic guess about how much it's going to cost.

In fact, that's a pretty good general rule for establishing market value: the less sure you are, the more conservative you should be. If there's a row of identical houses, all in good condition and two of them have sold for a certain price within the last six months, you can be pretty confident of what one of the others should be worth today. The further you depart from that ideal situation, the larger the margin you can be wrong by.

If a property really does seem to be offered at a bargain price, remember the rule: nobody gives a property away cheaply because they're feeling generous that day – only because there's a reason (often being in a rush) that's forcing them to drop the price. Have a re-read of the "What BMV isn't" section, and look out for anything else that could be holding its "real" value down. I'm not saying that you'll never get a bargain handed to you on a silver platter, but it's far more common that, contrary to initial appearances, it isn't such a good deal when you get down to it – so a little skepticism is always healthy.

Does the price work for you?

I said at the start of this chapter that I consider a property to have two prices: its market value, and the price at which it makes sense for *you* to buy it. We've talked about how to determine the market value, but what about determining your own price? Well, that's determined by your goals – another reason why you can't make well-informed buying decisions if you don't have a goal in the first place.

In the context of buy-to-let, you could express your goals for the acquisition in a few different ways: a certain yield, a certain ROI, a certain amount of monthly net profit to add to your bottom line. There could also be secondary goals, such as wanting a certain ROI *and* the ability to add value so you can remortgage and pull out cash later.

In the context of buy-to-sell projects, your goal is almost always to make a certain amount (or percentage) of profit – so you'd need to acquire the property, do any refurbishment work and build in your profit margin for less than the property could comfortably be re-sold for. Again, there might be secondary goals like concluding the project within a certain amount of time.

I'm not going to bash you over the head about the importance of having goals, but consider yourself lucky that I'm in a pacifist kind of mood today because I really should: *knowing what you want to achieve with a purchase is critical*. Without knowing what you want to achieve, you can't possibly know the maximum price you should be paying. If you *do* know what you're ultimately aiming for and how you want to get there, you can see how each individual purchase fits into that picture and decide whether any given opportunity moves you closer to your goals or not.

For example, if your goal is to make £3,000 per month in rental profit, you might set the strategy of buying ten properties, each making a net profit of £300, and each property must offer the possibility to add value and refinance because otherwise you'd run out of cash before buying all ten. With that strategy firmly in mind, imagine if the opportunity comes along to buy a property below market value, but it only makes £150 profit. Or perhaps it makes £350, but there's no potential to add value. That property won't move you closer to achieving your goal, so you'll say no.

Failing to take this approach means you could end up with a collection of perfectly well-bought properties, but still not end up where you want to be. There are worse fates in life of course, but surely you want to know that all this effort is going to pay off at some point?

OK, that probably counts as bashing you over the head – but it really is important.

Stacking the deal: buy-to-let

When you're buying a property to rent out, your primary goal will be in some way related to the amount of money the property generates over and above its costs. Whether you express it in terms of net yield, ROI or a cash figure, it all amounts to the same thing: how much am I left with after the rent has come in and all my bills have been paid?

Clearly, answering that question involves knowing two things:

- How much rent is going to come in?

- What are the costs going to be?

You'll probably have a rough idea of how much rent a property will achieve because you've been researching your area, but in the next section we'll get into more detail on how to estimate both the rent and how much rental demand there'll be.

That's the easy bit. Pinning down the expenses is a little more tricky, because the only certainty is that you'll be wrong: you can't possibly know in advance exactly what every last expense will be. Some try *really* hard to know, however – and they write to me asking what the typical insurance is on a two-bed flat, or how often to replace the carpets so they can amortise it over the right number of years in their spreadsheet.

I admire these people's spirit, because (a) spreadsheets rock, and (b) it's vital to get the numbers right so you're not disappointed by the returns you make. But given that life is short and the only certainty is that you'll be at least somewhat wrong, I just aim to make sure I'm wrong in the right direction. In other words, I make broad but pessimistic estimates of all costs so it's likely that the reality is going to be better than I expected.

Let's have a quick run-through of what your major costs are likely to be in a buy-to-let scenario:

Mortgage repayments. This is almost always going to be your largest single cost. Luckily, determining what the repayment will be is easy: take the amount you're borrowing, multiply it by the interest rate, and divide by 12 to get the monthly figure. (That's for an interest-only mortgage. For repayment the maths is beyond me, so Google "repayment mortgage calculator" and you'll find tools put together by people who did more than just scrape through their GCSE maths.)

The interest rate will probably change at some point during your ownership (even if you go for a fixed rate at first), so you'll want to "stress test" the purchase against a higher rate. The long-term average base rate in the UK is 5%, and typical variable-rate mortgages are priced at 2% above base, so you may want to work off a 7% repayment rate. However, the Bank of England has released a report saying that (paraphrasing a bunch of fancy maths) it doesn't expect the base rate to exceed 3% even in the long term, so you may be happy stress testing against 5% (to incorporate the typical 2% lender margin) instead.

Service charge and ground rent. If you're buying a flat, there'll be a service charge and ground rent to pay. The service charge will be determined in part by the facilities that need to be maintained (so if there are lifts, extensive grounds or a swimming pool, the bill will be higher than a bog-standard block), but also by how tight a rein the management company keeps on their costs. Even service charges for blocks with identical facilities can vary widely, so find out what the current costs are before running your numbers – although remember they can change over time, of course.

With flats there are also cyclical "major works" bills to contend with (such as repairs to the roof), but we won't worry about that for now.

Maintenance. This is the most unknowable expense of all. The only real "rule of thumb" I can give you is that maintenance costs are generally (very generally) lower in flats than houses. This is because many of the things that you might have to fork out for in a house (like replacing a cracked gutter) will be covered by your service charge in a flat. But, whether house or flat, there are plenty of impossible-to-estimate potential expenses. Will the boiler blow up on day one of your ownership or last for a decade? Will you have a leak in the bathroom that involves ripping everything apart and re-tiling at great expense? You just don't know, although insurance (which we'll talk about briefly later) can help to smooth out some of the bigger expenses somewhat.

Management. If you don't want to manage the property yourself, a management fee will typically set you back 8–15% of your rent. Some landlords consider this tantamount to highway robbery, but I'm not one of them. If you ask me, £50 (on a £500 rent) is worth it if it saves even one hour of my time per month – which it almost always will. But I digress.

Insurance. Not a major expense, but you need to make a small monthly allowance for buildings insurance – unless it's incorporated into the service charge of a flat.

Voids. At some point your property will be empty (even if it's just a small gap to change over between tenants), and it makes sense to factor that into your figures. Again, it's somewhat unknowable: even if demand is through the roof and you should in theory be able to just have a few days' gap to clean and attend to some maintenance, you might get a difficult tenant who refuses access for viewings during their notice period and leaves you needing a month to get someone else moved in.

Bills. As a very general rule, bills tend to be included as part of the rent in HMOs (sometimes with a cap or fair use policy), and not in single lets. If you're planning to include them, they (of course) need to be reflected in your calculations – not forgetting council tax, unless all occupants are students.

(I haven't forgotten that tax is a cost, and we'll be giving tax its own chapter later on.)

Knowing your anticipated rental income and having estimated your costs, you're in a position to assess the deal based on your criteria.

My preferred measure, because it's the most detailed, is ROI – the annual profit from holding an asset divided by the cost of acquiring the asset. The rent you can charge and the costs you incur are pretty much beyond your control (other than making improvements that allow you to increase the rent, or self-managing to cut out agency fees), which means it's *the price of acquiring the asset* you need to manipulate if you want to hit a certain ROI figure.

For example, say your ROI target is 8%. By knowing the rental income and all your costs (including the percentage of the purchase price you'll borrow and at what interest rate), you can pop everything into a simple spreadsheet and play with different purchase price figures until 8% ROI is the result. This way, you can determine the maximum amount you should pay for a property to make it work for you – *and you don't even need to know its market value.*

The market value is a factor, of course, because you only want to be paying the lower of the market value or the price that works for you. So even though you *could* afford to pay (say) £128,000 for a property and hit your ROI target, if you assessed the market value at £120,000 then you wouldn't want to go any higher than that.

If, however, the market value was £150,000 and you had the chance to buy it for £135,000, in theory you'd turn down that opportunity because £135,000 is higher than the £128,000 that works for you – although in reality, you may relax your ROI criteria to get the benefit of £15,000 of instant equity.

Gauging rental demand

If you're buying a property to rent it out, you'll obviously have two critical questions in mind:

- Will it rent?

- If so, how much for?

Rental markets change over time and often move cyclically throughout the year (especially in towns with a large student population), but they don't change *that* much or that fast. With a bit of research, you should be able to estimate the monthly rent you'll achieve to within £50 (meaning that if you assume – for the purpose of your calculations – that the rent you achieve will be in the middle of that range, you'll get nothing more than a nice £25 surprise or a philosophical £25 shrug of the shoulders).

Something of a side-note here, but rents are driven largely by wages (and also by local supply and demand). It makes sense: the amount each individual will be willing and able to spend on rent is going to be a proportion of their take-home pay. For that reason, rents are a lot less volatile than house prices, and will tend to drift up or down rather than spike suddenly. (House prices are driven by many different factors, which we'll explore when we talk about the property cycle in Part 3.)

Just to be clear: rents are determined by wages and local supply and demand – *not by landlords*. You can't decide to just stick the rent up by £100 a month because you feel like it or because your mortgage payments have increased. OK, you might have an exceptionally pliant tenant and there's a degree of lock-in because moving is a pain, but wouldn't *you* go elsewhere if you could get an equivalent product for £100 per month less?

In other words, you can try your luck with a rent at the high end of the market or try to get it let quickly by pricing at the low end, but demand isn't elastic enough for you to just set whatever price you like. This is why I get annoyed when the response to anything that increases the cost-base of landlords is "They'll just put up the rent and the tenant will end up paying for it": it's just not true, because the private rented sector is too fragmented for landlords to operate in a cartel in this way.

Anyway, where were we?

Ah yes: will it rent, and how much for?

Finding out the answer to both questions isn't much different from determining a property's market value – with the exception being that there is (unfortunately) no database of rental prices that have been achieved in the past. Instead, you have to work from the rents that are *advertised* – equivalent to working from an asking price – which isn't ideal, but rents achieved tend not to deviate that much from rents sought.

The process is quite simple and the considerations are the same as we saw when assessing house prices: fire up Rightmove or Zoopla, and search for properties to rent that are *nearby, equivalent in size* and *equivalent in quality*. On both sites you can tick a box to also see properties marked as "let agreed", which you should do to gather the most information possible.

My process isn't as geeky as you might think: I just search within a 1/4 mile of the property I'm interested in, sort in price order, and eyeball the data to see what kind of price range there is. From there, I click into different results to see what seems to separate those at the high end from those at the low end.

With exceptions caused by landlords trying their luck or agents not really knowing the correct value, the patterns are pretty obvious: rents are higher for bigger properties than smaller, good condition than mediocre condition, furnished than unfurnished, facilities in the building than none (in the case of flats), and parking than none. There's also a premium for locations that are well placed for transport links.

It's worth noting that specific pros and cons of the property affect both the price and the time it takes to let. For example, in a block of identical flats, the one on the ground floor with a view of a brick wall or noise from people slamming the door of the main entrance will take longer to rent (or need to be done so at a lower price) than the others. Things like funky layouts or unusual room sizes will put people off too. This kind of factor is hard to determine when looking at comparables online (because the photos on rental listings are often somewhat lacking), but it's important to take into account when you're deciding what to buy. Basically, all else being equal, a property with some kind of oddity or drawback will cost you on the rent or take longer to find a tenant for.

While you can get a pretty good idea from looking online, the best way to find out what a property will rent for (and how quickly) is to call up and ask some local agents. Online, it's hard to get an accurate idea of timescales: while you can see how many days ago a listing was added, you don't know for sure that it's truly still available. For example, sometimes agents leave one listing up for ages because they've got multiple units in that block with one listing counting for all of them, or they just plain forget to mark it as "let agreed".

You might be dubious about whether agents will tell you the truth, but if you call a few you'll probably find that there's a fairly accurate consensus – and if you get one who's particularly clueless or puffed-up and claims they can rent it in minutes for hundreds of pounds more than anyone else, they'll quickly stand out as an outlier. Letting agents don't have a great reputation, but they do see hundreds of properties each year. As a result, they're all too aware of the ones where they struggle to get people through the door, compared to the ones where the phone never stops ringing the minute they put them up online.

Stacking the deal: buy-to-sell

How do you gauge whether a potential buy-to-sell project stacks up or not? We'll discuss trading property in more detail in Part

3, but while we're talking about assessing deals, it makes sense to touch on them here briefly too.

Just as with buy-to-lets, you're going to be looking at two things: what price you should pay to give yourself a profit, and the demand for the final product. In this case though, of course, the "demand" you're concerned with isn't rental demand but people who'll want to buy the property from you once it's finished.

There are three main variables that you have some degree of control over:

- The price you buy it for

- The amount you spend on it

- The price you sell it for

And naturally, you make a profit when the price you sell it for is greater than the price you buy it for plus the amount you spend on it. We'll come back later to how much of a profit is "enough", but professionals generally look for at least 20% (e.g. spend a total of £100,000, sell for at least £120,000). This is decent compensation for your hard work, and also means that if everything goes horribly wrong you should still at least break even.

The variable you have the most control over is the price you buy it for, so it makes sense to stack the deal by working back from the final selling price – something you have *some* degree of control over (by appointing the right agent and staging it well), but which is ultimately determined by the local market.

Calculating the final selling price is accomplished in the same way as working out the market value of a potential buy-to-let property – the only difference being that whatever the state of the property now, you're interested in the price of comparable properties that are in mint condition. The same rules apply – only very nearby properties of the same size and with similar features are true comparables – and again, speaking to agents is very helpful indeed.

It's extremely important at this point to be conservative with the final sale price you think you can achieve – because if you calculate your figures based on a price that's £10,000 more than you can realistically achieve, that's £10,000 of profit that vanishes. You should also bear in mind that you're not in the position of an owner-occupier who can keep a property on the market for years until someone comes along, falls in love with it and is willing to pay an over-inflated price. You need to get your money out and move on, so ideally you want to be pricing it just below what's being asked for similar properties to generate interest and shift it quickly.

The amount you spend on the property is the most difficult part to determine if you don't have construction expertise yourself. I won't get into *how* to work it out at this point, but getting a realistic/pessimistic figure is crucial. A contingency of at least 10%, preferably 20%, is always a good idea because you never know what unexpected problems you'll discover until you start.

Weirdly, the less work you're doing, the more margin there is for error: if you know you're going to have to rip the house back to brick and start again, there's not much more that can go wrong.

In addition to the actual construction costs, there'll be all the other expenses that go along with buying and selling houses: legal fees, borrowing costs (if you're not using all your own cash), surveys, estate agents' fees, and everything down to insurance, council tax and utility bills for the period that you own it. Everything needs to be factored in.

With all of this calculated, you can work out the price you should be paying for the property in the first place: the final sale price, minus your costs, minus your desired profit margin:

Price you're willing to pay = final price you can sell it for - costs - desired profit margin

As you can see, the price you should pay for the property has precisely nothing to do with the asking price (or the "guide price" in an auction). Taking this approach is what separates the professionals from the amateurs: an amateur will knock 10% off the asking price and think they've got a great deal, then realise after toiling away for six months that they've spent much more than they imagined and will never be able to turn a profit. (Frustratingly, this means that you'll frequently find yourself being outbid on development opportunities by amateurs who are willing to pay more than really makes sense – which doesn't ultimately help them, but sucks for you too.)

So, say you've found a property you can secure for a price that allows you to make a nice 20% margin – even after being conservative on the resale price, and building in a healthy contingency for your costs. Snap it up, right?

Whoa there – we haven't yet considered the "demand" part of the equation… will anyone want to buy the final product?

Although you might have a niche in selling to investors looking for a buy-to-let opportunity, the majority of the time you'll be selling the property on to someone who wants to occupy it as their home. In this respect you're plucking the property out of one market – one populated by investors – and plonking it in a market of owner-occupiers who are only interested in "finished" properties that they can move straight into.

Is the owner-occupier market buoyant in the area surrounding your target property? This is a critical question, because you want the property to shift quickly at a good price. As we saw when we were talking about bridging finance, the costs rack up quickly each month – and even if you're using your own money, there's an "opportunity cost" to having it tied up in this project where it's not earning you a return (and you're still footing the council tax, insurance and utility bills).

The best way to find out, yet again, is to talk to local estate agents. Yes: some will try to put a gloss on things, but they still know what's what on their patch. Asking questions like "How many weeks on average is it taking to get an offer?" and "How many viewings on average is it taking to produce an offer?" will give you an insight.

You can supplement this with online research on two fronts. Firstly, on Zoopla, you can click "Agents" in the top menu and enter a postcode to bring up a list of all the agents who are registered with the site and operate in that area. Next to each one it has "Average sale listing age" – which tells you how long their listings typically sit on the site for. (Bear in mind that the property will stay there for the entire conveyancing process until the transaction finally completes.)

Also, by using a browser extension like Property Log for Chrome (which cleverly scrapes the Rightmove database and inserts extra information into each listing), you can see the history of individual properties. These tools will show you the date each property was listed and the date that it was marked as "Sold STC" (meaning that an offer was accepted and the conveyancing process started), which of course is exactly what you want to know. There's going to be a lot of individual variation because you don't know which properties had unrealistic vendors, rubbish agents and so on, but by looking at enough properties you can build up a picture.

For me, resale is the absolute key to flipping properties: it's the difference between being able to use the same funds to do one deal per year or two, and the difference between six months of finance costs or nine. Given the choice between a smaller potential profit in an absolute slam-dunk location or a bigger potential profit in a slightly more marginal area where you need a bit of luck, I'd take the former every time.

Chapter 10

The buying process

In this chapter we'll cover the whole process of buying a property, from the initial viewing to collecting the keys when the deal is done.

What you can't see on the page is the number of grey beard hairs I now have, as a direct result of going through this process myself. But don't worry: you'll have your own before long, because buying a property in England and Wales is *nuts*.

(If you live in Scotland: congratulations! You guys seem to have got it pretty much sorted. This chapter doesn't cover the Scottish legal process, but feel free to read along with an ever-increasing sense of smugness.)

The bonkers-ness of the whole situation comes from the fact that you need to make an offer on the basis of *nowhere near* enough information, incur a load of costs in finding out the full story… then if you still want to go ahead, potentially find that the vendor has changed their mind because nothing is binding until contracts have been exchanged.

So the process itself makes no sense, and it isn't exactly helped along by the cast of characters you'll encounter:

- An estate agent, whose strengths don't necessarily lie in the conveyancing process – and who has a million other things on the go in any case.

- A lender (and their surveyor) who is similarly stretched, and holds all the cards: even though they may have lending targets to meet, it isn't really any skin off their nose if this transaction doesn't happen.

- Solicitors, who remain a mystery to me and every investor I've ever spoken to. Key character traits include being out of the office, writing tetchy letters to each other, and just plain failing to do anything at all unless badgered endlessly.

- A vendor, who can find the whole situation "emotionally charged" if we're being polite, or just be plain crazy if we're not.

- You. You think you're perfect, but you're probably just as irrational and inefficient as everyone else. Sorry.

In short, it's a collection of humans with often opposing interests who need to carry out a complicated process with large sums of money at stake. It was never going to be easy, was it?

So now would be an excellent time to take up meditation, find religion, or do whatever it takes to become at peace with delays, setbacks and disappointments. Maybe I'm over-egging it some-what, but I think it's important to realise that the buying process is *hard work*. Sometimes, you'll even have a deal irreparably fall apart somewhere along the way – possibly after spending lots of time and money on it. Be prepared for the worst, and maybe (just maybe) you'll be pleasantly surprised.

Viewing the property

So far, you could have done all your research without leaving your desk (assuming you've got the postcode and a few internal photographs). In most cases at this stage, you'll probably want to go and kick a few bricks before you take things any further.

Why "in most cases"? Because if your approach is to be hands-off, you might decide not to visit at all. If you're buying through a sourcing company, it probably won't be an option anyway. And I own several properties that I've never been inside, be-cause I bought them via trusted contacts and I frankly couldn't be bothered to go there and see what I'd already seen in photo-graphs.

Most people will tell you that this is supremely risky, and they're right – it can be. By not viewing, you're relying purely on someone else's word: the photos might look great, but had they cropped out the industrial waste site next door, or neg-lected to show you the crumbling rear elevation? For that reason, you should research like crazy the person or company who's presenting the opportunity to you. If you trust them as much as you trust yourself, all good.

But let's be real here: viewing is better than *not* viewing if you've got the option. The investors who secure the best deals view a *lot* of properties: it wouldn't be uncommon for someone to view 50, make serious offers on five and end up buying just one. They'll keep on doing viewings even after they've seen hundreds of properties in their local area and will pretty much know from the address what they're going to see. Why do they bother?

Because as well as being able to see what works need doing and mentally cost it all up, viewings aren't just about the property itself – they're about building relationships and gathering in-formation. The more time you spend with an estate agent or auctioneer, the more likely they are (if they like you) to give you advance notice of something that's about to come onto the market. They'll also tell you more in person than they would over the phone about the vendor's situation, which is critical: you might value a property at £80,000, but is it worth a £10,000 discount to the vendor if they can shift it next week?

So if hands-off is your thing, no problem. But given that most people will want to view before they buy, let's look at what you want to have on your mental checklist as you walk around.

Location factors

- Where is it? In other words, how does it fit into the overall geography of the town or local area? Is it in an established residential area, or right in the thick of things, or a bit out of the way?

- Where are the nearest shops? Clearly this is something that tenants or buyers would care about, so local shops are good – but next door to a kebab shop isn't.

- What are the transport links like? Again, this is a major concern for most tenants and buyers. Proximity to train, bus or major road links make a huge difference to price and demand. But having a bus stop *directly* outside isn't great from a noise and litter point of view, and nor is having a house that shakes every time a train goes past.

- What is the parking situation? This matters more for some areas and demographics than others. It's particularly important for HMOs (where you might have five tenants with a car each), except in places like London where people tend to rely on public transport.

- How busy is the road? Lorries and boy racers using the street as a cut-through will be a turn-off.

- What are the conditions of surrounding houses like? You can tell a lot about the demographics of an area just by looking at front gardens and peering (in a non-creepy way) through a few windows.

- What can you tell about the area from sitting in your car for ten minutes observing comings and goings? Do you see a lot of people in suits getting home from work? Or groups of children hanging around? You can also make inferences about the neighbours from the cars that are parked. This all sounds very judgemental, but it's not about determining whether a street is "good enough" for you, the above-it-all property investor. Instead, it's about whether it's appropriate for your target market: realistically, there are streets where your target market will feel comfortable and others where they won't. For some people, children playing in the street on their bikes is a positive – for others it could be annoying or intimidating.

Condition factors

- Does the property appear to be structurally sound? You're not an expert and that's fine, but you can look for obvious slope and cracks. If it's a house, I tend to look at the lintels of the upper-floor windows from across the road to see if they're straight.

- Does the roof seem to be in good repair? You may or may not be able to see missing tiles from the front or the back. You can also see how much (if any) of the roof is flat, which tends to require more upkeep.

- Does it appear to have been extended? If so, you'll need to get your solicitor to check later whether it had the necessary consents. If not, are neighbouring properties extended – indicating that it would be possible to do so yourself if you wanted to add value?

- If it's a flat, what is the condition of the communal areas like? This is something beyond your control, but it will nevertheless impact on how desirable the property is, so it's worth taking note of.

- Is there double glazing? This will affect your assessment of the property's value, and tell you whether you need to budget for adding it yourself.

- How many bedrooms and bathrooms are there? Obviously.

- Is there the potential to reconfigure to add rooms or improve use of space? You could sketch a quick floorpan, or just look out for how you might be able to squeeze in an extra bedroom or en suite without making any of the rooms too cramped.

- Is there central heating? If so, does the boiler appear to be new or ancient? I'm no expert about these things, but I'll sometimes take a quick photo of the boiler to work it out from the model number afterwards.

- From looking at the consumer unit, what can you tell about the state of the electrics? Even if you're clueless about these things, snap a photo and you can show it to an electrician (or ask in a forum) later.

- Does the kitchen need updating? This is very much relative to your intended purpose. It might not be your style, but would it work for a rental property? Could you jazz it up just by changing the cupboard doors?

- Does the bathroom need updating? Again, what's "good enough" depends on your plans. You can get an idea of what the competition is like just from the photos on Rightmove and benchmark from there.

- What is the general decorative condition like? You won't necessarily know whether the wallpaper will take a new coat of paint without peeling or whether the whole thing will need replastering, but try to get as much of an idea as you can.

- Are there any obvious signs of damp? Using your nose is a good way to tell, as well as looking out for telltale black patches – especially on external walls and around windows. If you can smell something and you're suspicious, look behind strategically positioned furniture too...

Situation factors

- If it's a flat, what is the service charge and ground rent? This makes all the difference to the world to your ROI, so you can't make an offer without knowing.

- If it's a flat, how many years are left on the lease? Again, this is critical – so if the agent seems unsure on the matter, push them to find out and get back to you.

- Who lives there now? Is it rented out, and if so, will the property be vacant when you buy it? Does the vendor live there now, and if so do they have somewhere to move to? Is it empty, and if so, why – has the owner recently died, or has it just been vacated for sale, or has it just been refurbished?

- Why is the vendor selling? An honest answer is hard to come by (the agent is unlikely to say "To be honest, they need to sell by the end of the month or they're stuffed so they'll accept any price"), but you'll never know less after asking. You can also look out for telltale signs like "do not use" tape over toilets and sinks, which normally signals a repossession.

- How long has it been on the market? Agents are often either deliberately vague about this or just don't know, but it's worth asking – and you can look out for indications like a huge pile of post behind the door or waist-high grass.

- Have there been any offers yet? In agent lingo, "We've had a lot of interest" means "No". They'll sometimes tell you about offers that have fallen through because it helps to explain why it hasn't sold yet.

The circumstances surrounding the sale are the most valuable things you can find out – and because the agent knows this, it's seldom easy to get straight answers. This is why building relationships is a long-term game that's worth playing. Agents are only human (believe it or not), and as they get to know and like you they won't be able to help themselves from letting more slip.

Offering and negotiating

Once you've viewed the property, you should have a firm idea of the two numbers we talked about earlier: what it's objectively worth, and what it's worth to you. Your maximum offer should be the lower of those two numbers.

(If it needs refurbishing, then calculating these numbers can be tricky if you don't have experience. If possible, ask a builder to view the property with you and give a rough quote – but if that's not an option, your offer will just need to be highly conservative.)

Of course, you don't start by making your maximum offer: instead you want to make an offer that gets rejected. You read that right. Here's why:

In a negotiation you can never go backwards. If you make an offer and it's accepted immediately, it means you *could* have gone in lower. It's too late to do anything about it now though, because the vendor knows that you're actually willing to pay that amount – so backpedalling won't work. By having your first offer rejected you can satisfy yourself that you're not going in too high, and also "anchor" the conversation around your number. Even if the vendor is mortally offended by your offer of 40% below their asking price, somewhere in the back of the mind they'll start to question whether, hey – if that's the number you came up with, maybe it's also the number that everyone else will come up with and their own valuation is way off base.

When it comes to making the offer itself, some people prefer to make a formal written offer (email is fine) in a set format, while others are happy to do it verbally. There's an argument that putting it in writing makes you appear more serious and avoids the potential for misunderstandings, but I'm not convinced that it really matters either way.

What you *should* remember when making your offer is that a negotiation is about more than just the price. The other key factors are *certainty* and *speed* – so if you have these in your favour, you should make this clear in your offer. You'll then be a more attractive prospect to the vendor, especially if these factors are of particular importance to them.

In terms of certainty, you need to demonstrate that you're the kind of person who can be relied on to get the deal done. It's not just about attitude though: at a minimum, you should also be able to show proof of funds for the deposit and a decision in principle from a lender. The agent and/or vendor will still be aware that plenty could go wrong, but showing that you're financially prepared means your offers will be viewed more favourably than someone who's unable to back up their offer with cash.

You'll naturally benefit from speed by not having another property you need to sell (chain-free is highly attractive to agents and vendors alike), but you'll climb even further in their estimations if you're not relying on a mortgage at all. This is why asking the "situation" questions at the viewing is so important: if you get the impression that the vendor is under pressure to sell quickly, an all-cash offer that's 10% lower than a mortgage-contingent offer may be the more attractive one.

So if yours is a cash offer and you can move quickly, make that clear when you're putting the offer forward: this isn't just an offer of 20% below the asking price – it's an all-cash offer of 20% below the asking price, with the intention of completing inside six weeks.

Still, however you put your first offer forward, it should be rejected – which is great, because you know you're below the vendor's lower limit, so now you can gradually work up towards your maximum price.

How you proceed from there depends on your attitude and how determined you are to get the lowest possible price. Personally, as long as the deal still stacks up, I'm always inclined to pay a little more than I suspect is the absolute bottom line just to get the deal locked down. I have a lot going on, and getting the deal done and moving on is more important to me than the money.

(And now I sincerely hope I never end up trying to buy a house from you.)

Other people view negotiation as a game, and they love the thrill of pushing for the lowest price they can. There's no right or wrong way, but you must be aware of the single fact that determines the outcome before you start: the person who *needs* the deal to happen *will* end up losing. In other words, the best negotiation tactic is to look like you're willing to walk away – and the easiest way to pull that off is to genuinely be willing to walk away.

I don't mean to make that sound easy, because it's not. If you *really* want to get started or secure your next property, but you have limited time for viewings and you've already missed out on three deals this year (maybe even after having offers accepted only to fall through later), it's extremely difficult to remain dispassionate. You might, of course, choose to take my view: what does it matter if you get chased a bit higher than rock bottom as long as the numbers still work? That's fine, as long as you absolutely *don't* give in to the temptation to relax your numbers by paying more than you should.

So what do you do if you reach your maximum offer and it's still refused? My approach is to leave the offer on the table, but make clear that I'm looking at other opportunities and may need to withdraw it if I get an offer accepted elsewhere. The passing of time casts the same offer in very different lights: it's easy for a vendor to be greedy when the property has just gone on the market, but it can look very different just a couple of weeks later.

Appointing a solicitor

Once you've had an offer accepted, it's time to appoint a solicitor to act on your behalf. Your solicitor will take care of gathering all the necessary paperwork, making sure everything is in order with the sale contract, and dealing with your mortgage company if necessary.

If you've found a solicitor who is a delight to work with in every way, treat that person better than you do your own mother. I've already made comments that will fail to endear me to any solicitors who are reading, but every single one I've worked with has been annoying in at least one respect.

Annoyances include being hard to get hold of, missing important details, and being overly combative and turning even minor points into point-scoring against the other side – but the most noticeable flaw is that they're *slow*. This is a major issue for you, because a transaction that would take four weeks if they were proactive could end up taking 12 – and the more time that passes, the more chance there is for the vendor to change their mind or for something else to kill your deal.

As far as I can figure out, the main challenge is that solicitors are working on a lot of cases simultaneously – the majority of which are stuck as a result of waiting for the results of searches or answers to questions they've asked of the other side. As a result, unless someone is leaning on them heavily to get something done, they'll be reactive rather than proactive – meaning that if they fail to get a response to a query they've raised, weeks could go by without them noticing.

In terms of finding a solicitor, referrals are (as usual) the best way – and asking local estate agents for their recommendations might not be a bad idea either. They'll have worked with every local firm, and will have some insights into who is quick and who really, really isn't. In general it's just a case of kissing a lot of frogs before you find someone you can work well with – although if you're buying a property with very specific circumstances (like a short lease, or requiring a very fast completion), you should seek out recommendations for specialists in that situation.

You'll want to obtain a fixed price quote for the transaction (most firms offer this by default), which will be dependent on the purchase price and involve an extra cost if the property you're buying is leasehold (because there's more work involved). While there isn't a perfect correlation between quality and price, I'd advise staying away from "sausage factory" companies with names like SuperCheapConveyancing4U.biz. It's likely that they'll be slow and lack specific expertise, and – because your case will be handled by multiple people – you won't be able to call and speak to a single person who's been following the situation closely. The difference in price is never going to be huge (especially compared to the total amount of money that's at stake), so in my opinion it's a corner not worth cutting.

Surveys

If you're using a mortgage, your lender will undertake a valuation survey of the property before formally approving your mortgage offer and releasing the funds. While lenders are more cautious now than they were in the mid-2000s (when they'd sometimes do a "drive-by" valuation rather than bother to go inside), their surveys are still somewhat cursory. They'll assess the property's value by comparing it to other properties that have sold recently (in the same way that we assessed the property's value for our own purposes earlier), and also give their opinion about how much rent the property could achieve.

The aim is to give the lender confidence that their money is safe – that you'll be able to meet the monthly payments based on the rent the property can achieve, and that if they need to repossess, they know how much they can sell it for. It's worth noting that unless they down-value the property from the proposed purchase price, they will value it *at* the purchase price: if the property is widely marketed and the vendor accepts your offer of £80,000, that by definition sets the market price. It's irrelevant that a slow market, the vendor being in a rush and your suave good looks have encouraged them to accept a low offer, and you believe the property to be worth £95,000.

So the lender will want to conduct a valuation survey for their peace of mind, but before matters get that far – as soon as you've had an offer accepted and instructed a solicitor – you'll need to decide whether to also carry out a more detailed survey for *your* peace of mind. Your survey will have no bearing on what the lender will offer you (their own valuation is all that matters), but it will investigate the condition of the property in more detail so you can be more confident that you haven't missed anything.

When it comes to surveys, you've got a few options. The most comprehensive is a full Building Survey (formerly known as a Structural Survey), which is only really necessary for old properties, listed buildings or those built using non-standard construction methods. The survey will look into concerns around damp, drainage, woodworm, timber condition and more. Alternatively, rather than undertaking a full Building Survey, you could instruct an expert (found via Google or the relevant professional body for that type of work) to conduct a specialist investigation into a particular aspect of the property's condition if you have some reason to be concerned – such as drains or damp.

A suitable middle ground for most properties is the HomeBuyer Report (with a typical cost somewhere around £300–£500), which inspects the main aspects of the property and comments on whether repairs are required to them immediately, at some point, or not at all. Because the surveyor is acting for you rather than the lender, they will also be able to make a judgement about what the property is actually worth in its present condition.

The downside of a HomeBuyer Report is that surveyors can sometimes tend towards covering themselves by commenting on every peril that could possibly befall a property, even if there's no sign that it might happen. Sentences like "There is no evidence that the house is about to fall down, but houses have been known to fall down in some situations so this must be taken into account" (OK, slight exaggeration) aren't overly helpful, and I've seen many buyers become freaked out when presented with a giant list of possible catastrophes and no way of knowing which are legitimate concerns and which are just backside-covering.

Another limitation is that the surveyor won't risk doing any-thing to damage the property (such as lifting up carpets to check for damp), and often won't be able to gain access to all areas. This makes a survey pretty useless (in my opinion) for purpose-built flats, because they won't be able to comment on the most expensive things that could go wrong, like the roof and the heating.

So is it ultimately worth it? For flats I'd say "no" unless you want reassurance or there's particular cause for concern, and "probably yes" for houses if you don't consider yourself to be experienced in matters relating to a property's condition. You might also find it useful as a sanity-check if you're buying without a mortgage: as a lender won't be conducting their own valuation to check that it's worth what you're paying for it, you could consider a survey to be worthwhile as a second opinion. In this scenario, the survey would also be a valuable bargaining chip: if it values the property at £5,000 less than you've agreed to pay for it, you've got a very good chance of getting that sum taken off the purchase price because the vendor will assume that any other buyer would come to the same conclusion.

If you do decide to get a survey done, you can either ask an estate agent for a recommendation or search the database of Royal Institute of Chartered Surveyors (RICS) members at **ricsfirms.com**. Once the report comes back, don't be afraid to call the surveyor if you have any follow-up questions: you're entitled to make sure you understand it fully, and they may be less circumspect on the phone than they were in the official report.

The legal process

We can't put it off any longer: let's take a deep breath and go through the full conveyancing process...

1. Your offer will be verbally accepted, and you'll give the estate agent (assuming you're buying through an agent) your solicitor's details.

2. The agent will write to all parties with confirmation of the price and any conditions of the offer.

3. You will give your solicitor's details to your mortgage lender (unless you're buying with cash), and the solicitor will act for you in the process of arranging that too. At this point your solicitor will send you a bunch of forms

to fill in, and you'll generally have to advance them a few hundred pounds or so to cover the costs of local searches.

4.   As we've seen, you might decide to undertake a survey before taking things any further.

5.   Your solicitor will request local searches for various matters like planning, flooding, contamination, the presence of mines, and other fun things.

6.   The vendor's solicitor will send over a draft contract, along with an information form completed by the vendor with answers to all manner of questions about the property. Your solicitor will check all this over, and "raise enquiries" of the other side.

7.   If the property is leasehold, your solicitor will request documents from the managing agent relating to the lease, the service charge accounts, and so on.

8.   If you're using a mortgage, the lender will instruct a valuation. Once they're happy with the valuation and the other circumstances surrounding the sale, they will issue a mortgage offer and your solicitor will go through it to check the terms.

9.   If the property is being sold with a tenant in situ, your solicitor should request a copy of the tenancy agreement and proof that the deposit has been protected in an ap-

proved scheme (we'll see more about deposit protection in the "Management" chapter).

10. Eventually, everyone will be ready to agree dates for exchange and completion.

11. In time for exchange, you'll need to send the agreed deposit (typically 10%) to your solicitor. On the date of exchange, they will send this to the vendor's solicitor – at which point you'll be legally committed to the purchase.

12. In time for the day of completion, you'll need to send your solicitor the balance of funds that aren't covered by your mortgage (so if you've got a 75% mortgage and you've already paid 10%, you'll have to transfer the remaining 15%). Your solicitor will draw down the mortgage, and transfer all the funds over to the vendor. At this point, the property is legally yours and you can collect the keys.

13. Your solicitor will submit a Stamp Duty Land Tax return, and update the Land Registry.

That's an abridged and non-comprehensive version of the process – and it will vary depending on the particular circumstances of the sale – but it's enough to give you the gist. There are two things to note about the process:

- The sequence above doesn't show the massive, honking great gaps that will open up at every possible stage given half a chance. For a mortgage-dependent transaction, 8–12 weeks is typical – and it could be longer if there's a chain involved or you're just plain unlucky. The more people you invite to the party, the more potential there is for delays – so you can expect a leasehold transaction of a tenanted property with a mortgage to take the longest, and a cash purchase of a vacant freehold property to be the fastest.

- If you're sharp-eyed, you might have noticed that nobody is legally committed to the sale until the point of exchange – almost at the end of the process. Yes: it's possible that you'll incur all the costs of searches, surveys, valuations and legal fees, only for the vendor to change their mind at the last minute – or you might need to pull out after something nasty is uncovered that means you don't want to go ahead anymore. (Once again, congratulations to the fine nation of Scotland who require all relevant information to be publicly available at the point of the property being offered for sale, and accordingly all bids are legally binding.)

There's not a great deal you can do about the second point. If it turns out there are plans to build a motorway at the bottom of the garden, or the lease is shorter than you believed, or there's a looming major works bill, or the tenant in occupation is on a protected tenancy, you have little choice but to attempt to renegotiate the price in the light of this new information and pull out if you can't obtain enough of a deduction to make it worthwhile.

It's immensely frustrating, but it's better to lose a few hundred pounds in costs than to push ahead with a property you wouldn't have bought if you'd known all the facts from the start.

Regarding the slowness of the whole process, the solution is to take control. Don't be unnecessarily bolshy and have unrealistic expectations, but also don't be afraid to check in with your solicitor regularly and put in calls to the estate agent. If done with suitable charm and reasonableness, you can turn the estate agent into an ally: they have a vested interest in getting the deal done so that they can get paid, and by showing that you're on top of things you can encourage them to ask their client to nudge their solicitor into action.

You might feel like you're annoying all and sundry, but being a pest can mean picking up the keys weeks earlier than you otherwise would have done. And as well as it being good to crack on so you can start making money, speeding things up also reduces the chances of something going wrong. Time is the killer of deals: the longer things drag on for, the more chance there is for the vendor to get greedy, change their mind, die... it sounds dramatic, but these things happen.

Leasehold and tenanted property

As if the legal process wasn't challenging enough, there are a couple of situations where there's even more to think about:

buying leasehold property, or a property that's being sold with tenants in occupation.

Leashold property

The most important factor to consider in the purchase of lease-hold property is the remaining length of the lease. Leases are issued for long periods (often 125 or 199 years, but sometimes as many as 999 years), and when that lease runs down to zero it will revert to the freeholder – meaning that the property isn't yours anymore and you have to give the keys back.

That's what "leasehold" means: you're effectively "renting" the property from the freeholder for a very long period of time. This sounds bad, but in practice the leaseholder has an automatic right to extend the lease so it will only expire if they don't notice it drop to zero or can't afford the cost of extending. The price of extending the lease is for you and the freeholder to agree on, but if you can't reach agreement you can insist on going to a tribunal – where a set formula will be used to determine the price.

The cost of lease extension increases dramatically once there are less than 80 years remaining, for reasons that I won't go into right now. And once there are less than 60-ish years remaining, it will become very difficult to get a mortgage on the property. Buying a property with a short lease can be a valid strategy for picking up a bargain because it's going to deter so many potential buyers, but it's something you need to go into with eyes open – so checking the length of the lease is critical.

If you want the least hassle, a remaining lease term of at least 125 years is beneficial: even if you keep it for an entire mortgage term of 25 years, you won't have any issues selling it because there will still be 100 years left. The vendor or estate agent should be able to tell you the length of the lease at the outset before you make an offer, and your solicitor will check it as part of the conveyancing process.

The length of the lease isn't the only factor that matters, because the lease document itself defines the entire relationship between you (the leaseholder) and the freeholder. If there are any onerous restrictions or obligations in there, it will affect your whole period of ownership – and may also cause trouble when you decide to sell the property.

For example, when I was buying a flat once, my solicitor flagged up something in the lease that seemed so trivial I didn't really understand what it meant (and I still don't now), but he arranged a "deed of variation" with the freeholder to get it amended. The clause in question would have had no practical effect during my ownership, but could have caused major problems when I came to sell the property. This is why, when buying leasehold property, you want to make sure your solicitor is experienced in this type of transaction.

Your solicitor will inspect the lease and ask the freeholder or their management company for a Leasehold Information Pack –

which relates to the finances of the block or development. This should include at least a couple of years of service charge accounts, so you can see what the level of service charge has been and confirm that the present owner is up-to-date with payments – which is important, because any liability will become yours once you're the owner. It will also include the full accounts for the development (which will allow you to find out if there's any kind of "reserve fund" or "sinking fund" in place to cover future major works), and the pack should confirm whether any items of major work are planned for the coming years.

Finally, the pack will tell you what amount of ground rent needs to be paid annually to the freeholder in addition to the service charge. As well as knowing what the ground rent is now, you should check the lease to see if it can go up in future: it's sometimes the case that the ground rent is "staircased" so the amount (for example) increases by a prescribed amount every ten years.

Tenanted property

If you were planning on renting out a property anyway, buying with tenants already in-situ can be a great bonus – it means you have income from day one, and don't have any of the expense or hassle that would otherwise be involved in preparing and marketing the property to let.

Because the vast majority of properties are sold with vacant possession, solicitors often won't know what needs to be checked when tenants are involved. So as part of the conveyancing process, make sure they see the following:

- The current agreement that governs the tenancy. If it's some form of protected tenancy (as opposed to a standard assured shorthold tenancy), you could have major issues with removing the tenant or increasing the rent. Even if it's an assured shorthold tenancy, the specific wording of the agreement could give the tenant rights that you're not happy with.

- The certificate that states where the tenancy deposit is registered. If the correct process hasn't been followed, this could have repercussions for you too.

- Rental statements showing that the tenant is up-to-date with their payments.

Then, when it comes to completion, your solicitor should make sure that any rent that's already been paid is apportioned to you. For example, if the tenant pays monthly in advance on the first of the month and you complete on the 15th, you should be given the rent that's already been paid from the 15th through to the end of the month as part of the completion transaction.

Then, once you've taken ownership, you're legally required to write to the tenant informing them that you're their new landlord, and give them an address in England or Wales where they can serve notices. This can be your own address, a "care of" address, or the address of your managing agent.

By default, you and the tenants will continue to be bound by the existing tenancy agreement: you'll just step into the shoes of the previous landlord – which is why it's important to see the agreement in advance so you know what you're signing up for.

You can either continue in this way or offer the tenants a new tenancy agreement that replaces the old one – bearing in mind that they're not obliged to accept it if they don't want to.

Whether you issue a new agreement or continue with the old one, make sure that the tenants change their standing order to direct all future rent payments to you – because if the money continues to go to the former owner, it could be very difficult to recover.

Chapter 11

Refurbing

My favourite thing about property investment is how there are so many different ways to approach it, depending on your personal strengths and preferences. For some people, knowledge of building work is that strength: they're able to spot projects that look tricky and put other people off, secure the property for a great price, then use their skills and contacts to get the work done quickly and cheaply.

I am not that type of investor. Of all the things I'm hopeless at, anything related to getting my hands dirty is probably the most pitiful of all. But I'm in good company, because I know lots of investors who are strong analytically and can raise capital, but are totally flummoxed when it comes to pricing up a refurb, putting a team together and managing the project through to completion.

So if construction is your area of expertise, I won't be able to tell you anything you don't already know. Instead, this chapter is geared towards investors like me – who need to survive the process of hiring tradespeople and getting the job done. Dealing with refurbs might never be your favourite part of the job (it isn't mine), but you shouldn't let that put you off completely: the most profitable opportunities are usually where there's some kind of refurbishment work that needs to be done.

Staying compliant

When doing any kind of work, it's important to know whether your plans will require approval in terms of building regulations, planning permission, or both. You'll obviously assume that permission is required for big projects like an extension or loft conversion, but you might not be aware that the government can ensnare smaller jobs in their legislative claws too.

Let's take building regulations first. They exist to make sure you adhere to safety standards when you want to:

- Put up a new building

- Extend or alter an existing one

- In the words of the government's planning portal, "Provide services and/or fittings in a building such as washing and sanitary facilities, hot water cylinders, foul water and rainwater drainage, replacement windows, and fuel burning appliances of any type"

The planning portal I just quoted from has a useful list of common projects that require building regulations approval: **planningportal.gov.uk/permission/commonprojects**.

If you're using a tradesperson, it's their responsibility to get approval from the building regulations department of the local authority, and they'll also be the ones to face a fine if they don't – although as the owner of the building you could be issued with an order to bring shoddy work up to standard at your own expense.

If the tradesperson is a "competent person" (meaning that they're a member of a trade body scheme, like FENSA for windows or ECA for electrics), they can self-certify that their work meets buildings standards without having to invite in the local authority to inspect the job afterwards. They will issue you with a certificate stating that the work is compliant, which becomes very important when you come to sell or refinance the property: I've had a mortgage application held up in the past because I'd installed new windows and the fitter had forgotten to give me the certificate.

Doing the work yourself? Then it's your responsibility to get approval before doing the works and have them signed off afterwards, so check the planning portal to see what you need to do.

Then there's planning permission. In addition to building regulations approval, you might also need permission from the local authority for projects that involve a new construction, extension, or a change of use.

Some projects will fall under "permitted development", meaning you don't need to seek permission. Again, the government portal's list of common projects (**planningportal.gov.uk/permis-sion/commonprojects**) will tell you if the project falls under permitted development or whether you need to apply for planning permission.

Even if the project appears not to require planning permission, it's still a good idea to contact the local authority to check before going ahead: you might be restricted for various other reasons. For example, the property might be in a Conservation Area, or the local authority might have issued something called an Article 4 directive, which means they've locally withdrawn certain permitted development rights that apply nationally.

Finding tradespeople

As I've said, I'm not the "hands dirty" type. My crowning DIY achievement is stopping a door from squeaking by spraying some WD-40 on it, and my wife didn't hear the end of what a genius I was for a week. As a result of my general hopelessness though, I've hired a fair number of tradespeople and can give you some pointers on how to do the same.

Finding a builder is no different from finding anyone else to perform a service for you: a personal recommendation trumps everything else, so ask around. Of course, you want a builder who's busy because they're good, but you're also not willing to wait because the property is costing you money the whole time it's empty – so start the process as early as you can. If you're buying a property, you can try to negotiate getting access after exchange and before completion to either price up the work or actually start doing it.

In the absence of a personal recommendation, I've had a lot of success using a site called My Builder (**mybuilder.com**) – where you can post a job for tradespeople to express an interest in. Other similar sites (such as Rated People and Checkatrade) are available and may have better coverage in your area, but that's the one I've happened to use.

The attraction of these sites is that past clients get to publicly rate and review the tradespeople they've hired via the site. While not as good as personal recommendation, it's a lot more reassuring than unchecked testimonials on a tradesperson's personal website. Where possible I try to only consider people with more than 20 reviews, with all but one of them positive – a little leeway is required because there are probably more crazy clients than cowboy builders out there. My Builder (and other similar websites) also require each tradesperson to submit current copies of their insurance and professional membership certificates to the site, so you can be reassured that their credentials are in order without any effort on your part.

For anything beyond the smallest job, the normal commonsense rules apply: get three quotes and trust your gut. To make sure you're comparing like with like, ask everyone to be clear about the exact scope of work: you might find for example that one quote is more expensive because the builder anticipates needing to replaster, whereas someone else has just assumed that the old plaster will be fine.

I always insist on a fixed price quote (rather than one based on how long the job takes) so I know in advance how much it will cost, and the builder has the incentive to get the job done and get paid rather than drag it out. I also ask for that quote to be broken down into labour and materials, which makes it easier to dig into the quote in more detail. Rather than just having someone suck air through his teeth, scratch his head and say "You're looking at about two grand there," you can ask how many days that includes for each trade at what day rate – making any padding in the quote immediately obvious.

When it comes to materials, I'm generally happy for the builder to supply the basics because they'll have access to better prices than I will – and although they'll often mark up the prices a bit to account for their time in doing the running around, it saves me doing it myself. For anything where personal taste is more of a factor, like a bathroom suite, you might prefer to supply your own.

Big jobs (which I'd personally classify as being anything over a couple of thousand pounds) deserve a contract with clear specifications, dates, figures and provisions for when things go wrong. The Federation of Master Builders has put together a template that you can just print off and fill in the blanks (**home-extension.co.uk/fmbcontract.pdf**).

Admin tends not to be the strong suit of many tradespeople, but anyone legitimate won't be averse to signing a contract: it's in their interests for everything to be clear too because as I said, the world isn't lacking nutty or unreasonable clients.

Even for smaller jobs where a formal contract is unnecessary, I tend to put everything in writing (just an email trail is fine) and get into a level of detail that's amused more than one builder in the past. But hey, clarity is important – you're hiring a builder, not a mind reader, so you can't complain if they fill in any gaps themselves and you don't like the end result.

Deciding on the spec

I feel like I'm patronising you by even mentioning this, but I feel I need to because people still get it spectacularly wrong: when it comes to a rental property, you won't be living there – which means you shouldn't impose your tastes and standards on the property.

Let's address standards first, because it's easy to succumb to over-speccing. Just because you'd be mortified to receive a guest and have them see that you use any paint other than Farrow & Ball, that doesn't mean it's necessary in a rental property – unless you're going for the exceptionally high end of the market. The same goes for elaborate kitchen and bathroom fittings: you can buy a tap for anything from a fiver to a fortune, and nobody is going to pay more than the market rent just because you've blown the bathroom budget.

The key is to let the market dictate what the standard of the finish should be. You can get a sense of what your market requires by looking at similar "let agreed" properties on Rightmove and seeing what they have in common, or by asking local landlords. If you're planning on using a letting agent to let or manage the property, invite a few agents over to give their opinion too. They see hundreds of properties per year and know exactly what makes a difference between the ones that "stick" and the ones that are snapped up as soon as they come on the market.

For example, an agent once saved me a small fortune with his market knowledge. I had a property complete while I was away on holiday, so I asked a professional project manager to go over and draw up a specification of the work needed. When the quote came back, I nearly choked on my Mai Tai: the figure was three times the guesstimate I had in my head and included recessed LED lights, replastering every ceiling, an expensive shower-bath… the works. It would have been the most fancy flat for miles around, but would it have made any difference to the rent I received? I thought not, so when I returned to the country I got a local letting agent over who confirmed that nothing so extensive was necessary.

As a result I fired the project manager, put a team together myself, and got the work done for almost exactly the figure I had in mind in the first place. True to the letting agent's word (which is possibly the first time that phrase has ever appeared in print), the property let on its second day on the market and hasn't been empty since. The lesson here is that even professionals are prone to over-speccing, and local knowledge is everything.

The other classic mistake is to impose your personal taste on the property, which is an easy one to fix: don't do it. If you look at the units owned by professional investors, they tend to look like identical beige boxes – which they are, because that's what rents fastest and creates the least hassle. Paint should be a variant of white, carpets should be beige or cappuccino, and ceilings should be absent of tacky pink plastic chandeliers (I have actually seen this).

Of course, tenants still want the property to feel homely – and if you're furnishing the property or staging it for viewings you'll find that little details go along way. You can create a dash of colour with cushions, and throw in the odd plant to make it look welcoming and help them to imagine themselves living there – but ultimately, bright and clean is all that anyone ever wants.

Overseeing the project

Depending on the size of the project and your own particular skill set, you might decide to manage the project yourself and hire in individual trades, or hire one main contractor to serve as project manager and sub-contract any jobs that they can't take on themselves.

If you choose to manage the project yourself, you'll need to have detailed knowledge of the construction process, as well as stellar communication and organisational skills. Being the project manager is a *massive* job – and if you don't have previous building experience, the thought of doing it probably scares the life out of you. There's a school of thought that says you should manage your first major job yourself – because you'll learn so much it will stand you in good stead for all future projects, even if you choose to hire someone else to project manage in future. I understand the logic, but clearly it's not something I subscribe to myself.

Even if you recognise your limitations (whether that's time or experience) and put someone else in charge, remember: you're still the boss. As with everything in life, the squeaky wheel gets the grease. The reality is that builders are usually juggling multiple jobs, and if you're not on top of them it's easy for your project to be the one that falls to the bottom of the pile. The jobs I've seen go the most wrong are the ones where the investor put someone in charge and expected to come back a couple of months later to a totally finished project. Instead, they tended to find that the builders had got as far as making everything a total mess, but stopped short of putting it back together again.

So, whatever the arrangement, make sure you're a constant presence. Be on the phone every day, and on site as often as you can. Don't get in the way or be prematurely aggressive, but do show through your actions that you're on top of things and will give them earache if things slip.

Overseeing the project also means keeping an eye on the time and the budget. Let's be real here: the likelihood is that your project *will* go over time and over budget. The solution is to make sure you've factored that in from the start.

In other words, if a job *absolutely must* be done in two months' time, agree with everyone involved that it needs to be done in a month. Even if everyone has the best of intentions and works as hard as possible, unexpected delays will always creep in. Whether it's weather, delays with materials or nasty complications arising, I'm yet to see a project of any size that runs exactly as you'd expect it to in an ideal world.

The same goes for the budget, because time and money are very closely linked when it comes to building projects. However carefully the job is specced out, legitimate unexpected expenses will crop up. (And just to be clear, it's not a legitimate unexpected expense to suddenly decide that the £20 light fittings just aren't fancy enough after all and you want to buy the £100 ones.)

The level of financial contingency you set is up to you, but I suggest 20%. It's on the pessimistic end of the scale, but that's the point: the absolute worst thing that can happen is to run out of money before you can finish, so you need to be able to cope with any reasonable eventuality.

Chapter 12

Management

When it comes to managing a property, you need to make a decision: are you a landlord, or are you an investor?

When I think of the word "landlord", I picture someone coming round on a Saturday morning to collect an envelope with the week's rent in it. If you report that the heating isn't working, he'll turn up with his mate from the pub and swear a lot in the vicinity of the boiler for an hour or two before mumbling something about coming back tomorrow with the right part. You will never see him again.

When I think "investor", I imagine... nothing – because when do you ever see an investor? She doesn't visit her properties to check up on tenants, or go to Astra Zeneca's HQ to make sure they're not doing anything that will affect her share price, or sit in the bank vault polishing her physical gold. She spots an investment case, allocates the resources, and lets other people take care of the day-to-day. In the meantime, she may or may not be letting out an evil chuckle while stroking a white cat.

Clearly, these are caricatures of the extreme ends of the spectrum. It's up to you where in the middle you want to fall – a decision that starts with deciding whether to self-manage or delegate responsibility to an agent. That's a contentious topic that we'll explore near the start of this chapter. If you choose to use an agent I'll provide some tips for finding a good one, and if you're self-managing I'll give you a list of everything you need to consider during the process.

This book is about property *investment*, not property *management* – so I won't attempt to tell you every last thing you need to know about managing a property. That would be a whole book in itself… and it's actually one that I've written: go to **property-geek.net/landlordbook** to find out more about my book, How To Be A Landlord.

It's a subject I know a fair bit about, both from taking professional management qualifications and the day-to-day experience of running Property Hub Lets. Here though, I'll just give you the "must know" stuff along with links to resources to find out more – because while good management is important, it's not something to get bogged down in.

Even if you decide to self-manage rather than using a letting agent, I strongly encourage you to apply the *investor mindset* to the task. There are all manner of jobs that other people can do on your behalf – from referencing potential tenants to dealing with repairs. There's nothing wrong with choosing to do these things yourself if you enjoy doing them, but you need to be aware that the more time you spend on *managing* the less time you'll have left over for *investing*.

Before getting into the ins and outs of property management, we first need to touch on something fundamental that property owners *must* understand. We throw around the word "tenant"… but what actually *is* a tenancy, and why does that matter so much?

What is a tenancy?

When you issue a tenancy, you're granting legal rights to the property that *supersede your own* for as long as the tenancy agreement lasts. If that sounds serious, that's because it is.

If you want to enter the property, you need to seek permission. If you want to get the property back for any reason – even if that reason is "they've trashed the house and haven't paid a penny in rent" – you need to follow a specific legal process. And if you made a mistake in the course of setting up or managing the tenancy, you may not be allowed to end the tenancy at all.

Issuing a tenancy, then, is very different from having a lodger, or allowing a friend to stay on your sofa, or even having a holiday cottage where there's a contract that allows the visitor to stay for a fortnight. Those are all contractual relationships rather than tenancies, so if you want the person to leave and they refuse, you could immediately attempt to get the police to remove them. Although I haven't tried it, this is what would happen if you refused to check out at the end of your stay in a hotel room.

Without getting into the boring ins and outs of tenancy law, the general rule is this: if you let out a property to someone who will occupy it as their main home without you living there at the same time, you've got a tenancy on your hands. Even if you issue a contract with "This is not a tenancy" written at the top (or have no written contract at all), the courts will still view it as a tenancy.

Rather than just scaring you for the sake of it, I'm bringing up what a tenancy really is to make two points that have a major bearing on the management of the property.

Firstly, under an Assured Shorthold Tenancy (AST) – the type that's now used in almost all cases in England and Wales – you have certain obligations as a landlord that can't be wriggled out of. These include providing facilities for heating and hot water, adequate drainage and sanitary installations, and maintaining the property so it's free of serious hazards. You must also give your tenant "quiet enjoyment", which means you need to give at least 24 hours' notice of visits to the property. These obligations are set in stone: even if you wrote something to the contrary in the tenancy agreement itself, a court would automatically side against you.

Secondly, and most importantly, the only legal way of removing tenants is through the courts. Broadly speaking, there are three ways in which tenants in England and Wales (Scotland has different laws and terminology) end up leaving a property:

- They leave voluntarily, either because they want to move on or because the landlord issues them with a valid "Section 21" notice and they comply. A Section 21 notice is a way of saying that the tenant hasn't done anything wrong but you want the property back at the end of the tenancy agreement anyway.

- They fail to leave after being issued with a Section 21 notice, so the court enforces the notice and evicts them if they don't comply. If (and only if) the law has been followed to the letter throughout the tenancy and in drawing up the Section 21 paperwork, the court will always rule in the landlord's favour – but the process can still take a couple of months.

- They cause so much trouble that the landlord wants to get rid of them, but can't use a Section 21 notice because the tenancy agreement is nowhere near ending yet. Instead, they issue a Section 8 notice – which requires them to choose one or more reasons from a pre-written list why they want the tenant to leave. In this situation the court won't automatically rule in favour of the landlord, so the whole eviction process can fall apart – and even if it succeeds, it can take months.

At the moment, the government is planning to remove the "no fault" (Section 21) eviction route and reform the Section 8 route instead. Details about when this will happen and exactly what will change are currently sparse, so keep an eye out for news.

The best way for tenants to leave, clearly, is by choosing to do so themselves or by complying with the landlord's request. This is how the vast majority of tenancies end – but when some kind of legal action is needed, the process can be *very* expensive, time-consuming and emotionally draining.

I'm making these points early in this chapter to emphasise the importance of putting good tenants into your property in the first place, and managing the tenancy correctly. With good tenants you'll have no need to ask them to leave – but if you do, they'll go quietly without dragging you through the courts. Even if you slip up and end up with a not-so-good tenant, managing the property correctly will make sure that any legal action won't fall down as a result of you failing to meet a legal obligation or botching the paperwork.

I've been trying to scare you a bit, but I don't want to go over-board. As I've already said, the vast majority of tenancies end happily. You might get unlucky every so often, but when you dig into the detail of most horror stories you hear, it turns out that the landlord has often done something daft – like let a friend move in without a written agreement, or failed to comply with legislation around safety or deposits.

So with a healthy appreciation of why it's so important to get things right, we can decide who to put in charge of those all-important details: should you use a managing agent, or do it yourself?

Should you self-manage or use an agent?

Some people get very het up about whether self-managing or using a letting agent is best. If that's you – maybe you think "all agents are useless rip-off merchants" or "there's no way I could talk to a tenant about not paying their rent without losing my rag" – I won't attempt to change your mind.

After all, there's no "right" answer – only the answer that's right for you. If you don't have a firm opinion already, making that decision comes down to three factors:

- How do you value your time? If you consider your time to be worth £100 per hour, then a letting agent's monthly commission of £50 (based on 10% of £500 rent) is a good deal as long as it saves you at least 30 minutes per month.

- What do you enjoy doing? Some people get a real kick out of fixing things and leaping into action to make tenants happy – and if so, that's worth taking into account even if it's not the best use of your time financially.

- How confident are you in your ability to successfully complete all the tasks that go along with letting and managing a property? The consequences of getting it wrong can be serious, so if you're not a detail-orientated person it might not be for you.

Of course, circumstances change over time. Many investors start using an agent then have a bad experience that causes them to take the properties back and do it themselves – or alternatively, they might start self-managing then get too busy and pass it all over. Far more important than making the "agent or not?" decision is to make sure you employ the *right* agent or self-manage *effectively* – both subjects we'll turn to next.

Seeing as you asked (or didn't, but now you've bought this book you're stuck with me), I'll give you my opinion: a *good* managing agent is an absolute bargain. Bear in mind, of course, that I own a letting agency so I'm not a disinterested party in this discussion.

For example, let's take a pretty typical 10% + VAT (currently 12%) management fee, which is £60 of a £500 monthly rent. As I said before, if I value my time at £100 per hour I only need to save a smidgen over 30 minutes per month for it to be a good deal. And personally, I put a massive premium not just on the phone not ringing – but on having *no possibility* of the phone ringing. There are a lot of things I love doing, and dropping everything to book an emergency plumber isn't one of them. Even if it's a bad financial deal (which I don't think it is), I'd still keep paying because having control over my time is more important than maximising my return.

This isn't a recommendation to use an agent – just an explanation of what I choose to do right now. When my portfolio was smaller and I had more time on my hands, I managed them myself – and that was the right choice for me at the time too.

With your decision made either way (or at least an understanding of the grounds on which to make that decision)... how *do* you find a managing agent, or alternatively, how *do* you manage a property yourself?

How to find a managing agent

It won't come as news that letting agents in the UK don't have the best of reputations – and by "don't have the best of reputations" I mean that the majority of the population view them as dishonest, charmless, incompetent, overcharging leeches.

And you know what? Many of them are. Bizarre as it seems, anyone can start up a letting agency in England without any qualifications or experience whatsoever – although legislation to regulate the industry has been promised, and is already in place in Wales and Scotland. Nevertheless, it's a dangerous situation for a property investor to walk into, because it's no easy task to separate those who just talk a good game from the ones who actually know what they're doing.

But appointing the right agent is critical because even if the agent has day-to-day control, *you as the property owner remain legally responsible* for everything they do. So if they fail to book in a gas safety inspection or "forget" to place the tenant's deposit in a recognised scheme, that's an "oops my bad" for them and potentially a massive headache for you.

How, then, do you separate the competent professionals from the sharp-suited charlatans?

- As ever, recommendations trump all. This is where local networking comes into its own: if you speak to a land-lord who's had multiple properties with the same agency for a number of years without complaint, you're onto a winner.

- Are they property investors themselves? It's no guarantee, but agencies that started off by managing the founder's own portfolio are often run along more profes-sional lines. If some of the staff are investors too, all the better – they'll understand your needs perfectly.

- Which online portals do they market your property on? Whatever they do locally, the reality is that almost all property searches (outside of specific niches) start on Rightmove, Zoopla or OnTheMarket.

- What's the quality of their marketing like? Take a look at their online listings and see if you'd be happy to have your property represented similarly to the ones they already have.

- The website All Agents (**allagents.co.uk**) allows users to submit reviews of agencies, so you can see what clients and tenants say about them. (Take tenants' gripes with a pinch of salt, because agencies are powerless if the landlord is unresponsive or unwilling to pay up for repairs.)

- Ask to see the agency's terms of business before taking them on. You'd be amazed how many agencies don't have written terms of business at all, which I'd take as a warning sign: how can you engage an agent without knowing the terms under which that relationship will operate?

- If not included in the terms of business, ask them for a full breakdown of all fees that will be charged to you. If they're at all evasive about this, I'd move on. It's important for you because a low monthly fee is meaningless if they sting you for extra fees at every opportunity.

- Ask if the agent is a member of a redress scheme, like The Property Ombudsman. If not, move on: it's been mandatory to be a member of such a scheme since October 2014, so if they're flouting that rule it doesn't bode well for them making sure you comply with your own legal requirements.

- Similarly, does the agent list their fees on their website and in their marketing material? This has been a legal requirement since October 2014 as well.

Those points are pretty unarguable ways to see whether or not you're dealing with a professional outfit. I'll also share some tips that fall squarely into the category of "personal opinion". They've worked for me, but others may disagree:

- Personally, I'd steer clear of the big national chains – such as a very famous one whose name, and former clients' reactions when you mention them, both start with an "F". While there's nothing wrong with chains as such, staff turnover tends to be high so you can find yourself dealing with someone different every time you call.

- Where possible, I'd favour a company that specialises in lettings over one that also does sales. That's because within agencies that do both, lettings is often seen as "second class". Sales is where everyone wants to be, and staff are only stuck in lettings until they can work their way up to a sales job. (Although this is changing as sales agents are under threat from lack of stock and online competitors, so lettings is coming to be seen as the "bread and butter" and treated more seriously.)

- You could award points to agencies who are part of a professional body like ARLA Propertymark, because it theoretically means that they need to abide by certain rules in order to remain a member. In practice, spot-checks by these bodies are few and far between so I don't see it as much of a guarantee.

- I'd have nothing to do with a company that pressures you by saying they have "qualified tenants waiting for a property like yours", or even goes so far as to ask if they can bring someone around to view before you've committed to working with them. These are nothing but sales tactics. If you've bought a property in a good rental location and it's of the right standard, *any* agent will be able to find you tenants and there's no need to jump at the first offer that comes along.

Even after following these tips to put a good agent in place, I still strongly recommend understanding at least the basics of lettings law and practice – because again, it's you who'll be on the hook for any mistakes, so it pays to keep an eye out for anywhere that they may have slipped up. And mistakes can happen: even if the company has come highly recommended and the owner is a property investor herself, you can't guarantee that they won't get busy and leave the 17-year-old Saturday boy in charge of drawing up your tenancy agreement.

Successful self-management

Self-management can be seen as a sliding scale. At one end, you've got what probably first comes to mind: doing every last thing yourself. If that's what you want to do, that's fine – but it's only one option.

At the other end, you've got what I used to do in my self-management days: retain overall control but outsource every individual job. It was still my phone number that the tenant was given, but whenever something needed to be done I instructed someone else.

Granted, by the time you've outsourced all the main jobs, the price difference between that and just paying an agent will probably be minimal – but if you prefer to keep hold of overall control, it's a way of escaping the binary choice of "do it all yourself" or "hand the whole thing to someone else".

In the middle of these two extremes, there's plenty of leeway: you can do the bits you want to do, and put someone else in charge of the rest. It's up to you where on the spectrum you want to fall – but my intention is to show you how to keep your focus on investing, and not let you get sidetracked by counting teacups or combing through an applicant's bank statements.

What can you outsource?

Finding a tenant. As I've already said, depending on the property's location you can probably find an agent to offer a "tenant find" service for the cost of around one month's rent. The alternative is to advertise the property on the portals yourself for £50–100 (via a service like OpenRent), but you need to see if you're still saving money after factoring in the cost of your time for doing all the viewings and administrative chores.

Referencing. Search "tenant referencing" and you'll find all manner of companies who will undertake a full reference for around £25. This typically includes checking their identity and verifying their current address, searching for adverse entries on their credit file, checking affordability, and taking up references with their employer and previous landlord. Why on earth would you choose to do that yourself instead of paying £25?

Inventory. A quality inventory (correctly known as an "inventory and schedule of condition") is absolutely essential. Without one, you'll automatically lose any claim to make a deduction from your tenant's deposit – because you'll have no record of the property's condition at the start of the tenancy. A good inventory is thorough, impartial, and contains plenty of date-stamped photos so there can be no arguments about its contents. If you don't fancy doing this yourself, just search for "inventory clerk [location]" – prices will start somewhere around £80 and depend on the size of property and level of furnishing. The check-out at the end of the tenancy can be outsourced to an inventory clerk too.

Repairs. I'd say that the most valuable members of your team are a reliable jack-of-all-trades handyman and a plumber/gas engineer: the most common problems I come across fall under the categories of leaks, hot water problems and "general stuff". Unless you're operating at the kind of scale where you can offer someone so much work they'll never fail to pick up the phone to you, finding someone reliable who's not busy when you need them is a constant challenge. If you don't already have the right person on hand when disaster strikes, I recommend using a site like **mybuilder.com** or **checkatrade.com**. You place your job, contractors bid, and you can see their reviews from previous clients to assure yourself that they're up to the task.

Bits and bobs. For those random tasks that require an in-person visit, there's normally a way to find someone else to do it. In London there's Airtasker, nationwide there's Gumtree, or you could try posting a request on a local Facebook group or message board. You could even decide to outsource periodic inspections in this way, by sending in someone armed with a simple checklist and ask them to snap photos on their phone of anything that looks important.

Rent collection

Rent collection isn't something to take a laid-back attitude about. Even if you've got plenty of breathing space between the date the rent comes in and the date your expenses go out, I recommend getting on the tenant's case the instant – not quite 12.01am, but as close as is socially acceptable – the rent due date has passed. You'll have tenants who are always going to be a dream and tenants who will always cause you trouble, but there are a large proportion in the middle who can easily go either way. If you fail to demonstrate that paying the rent is a non-negotiable ingredient in them having a quiet and pleasant life, it can easily slip down their list of priorities.

Call me heartless, but I really don't have any sympathy for late payment: I keep my side of the bargain in providing a good home and making repairs promptly, and I expect the tenant to keep theirs in paying the rent as agreed. I'm amazed by the number of landlords who accept erratic payment dates, part-payments around Christmas and an extra tenner a month here and there to reduce arrears. While in some sectors of the market it's probably a reality of doing business, in most cases it should be possible to find a tenant with the means and willingness to pay on time, every time. There's wanting to be understanding and recognising the fact that anyone can fall on hard times, and there's being a soft touch – and I genuinely think that more landlords than necessary fall into the latter category.

A nice option is to take payment by direct debit using **gocardless.com**. You send the tenant a link to set up the arrangement, you get confirmation that it's been set up, then – and here's the clever bit – you also get a notification if the arrangement is cancelled. The fee is £2 per payment, and is well worth it because it puts you in control: rather than wondering if a standing order has been set up or if it's been cancelled, you'll know exactly what's going on so you can take action before the rent just doesn't show up one day.

Communication

A lack of communication is where many landlord/tenant relationships fall down. If a tenant feels like they're not being listened to, they're more likely to leave and less likely to take pains to look after the property.

But there are limits. I don't recommend giving out your personal mobile number, nor taking calls outside office hours. If you answer the phone at 11pm once, you can expect more 11pm calls in future – even if the problem isn't urgent.

(I know I'm coming across as a heartless ogre in this whole chapter, and most tenants are great people who have no desire to unduly bother you or take advantage. But I think it's helpful for everyone to know where the line is drawn – and providing a good home doesn't have to mean being reachable on demand 24/7.)

Instead, I recommend either getting a separate phone number, or – better yet – using a professional call-answering service who can pass messages on to you. If you search for "call answering service" you'll find companies who will charge by the call (somewhere in the region of £1 each time) instead of a monthly fee – so it'll cost you very little.

Where possible, it's actually better to communicate by email. This isn't something that all tenants will be willing or able to do, but I consider it ideal because it doesn't interrupt whatever you were doing and it establishes a trail of proof in writing just in case it's needed. Again, set up a dedicated address that forwards to your main inbox. SMS and WhatsApp messages are fine too, but it's possible to lose all your historic conversations so make sure you take screenshots of anything important (like a message demonstrating that you've responded to a critical repair request in a reasonable timeframe).

Aside from the logistics of communication, the main *principles* of communication are to be responsive, professional and honest. You can find yourself having conversations about emotionally charged issues – like wanting to increase the rent, or the tenant having a difficult change in circumstances – and those conversations will be easier if you're clearly a decent human being yet aren't their best buddy. If a tenant isn't comfortable talking to you, they might end up withholding important information out of embarrassment or mistrust – which leads to worse outcomes when the truth comes out.

The management process

Whether you decide to use an agent or do it yourself, it's important to understand the main tasks that go along with managing a property. If you're self-managing, this section can serve as a checklist of what needs to be done. If you're using an agent, you can use it to make sure they're doing what they're supposed to do (and simultaneously be grateful that you don't have to do it yourself).

There's a heck of a lot of detail behind all of this – but as I've said, that's the subject of my book **How To Be A Landlord (propertygeek.net/landlordbook)**. Where more information would be useful, I've linked to the official UK government site. It doesn't cover every topic in massive detail, but you can at least be sure that it's been updated with any changes in legislation since your copy of this book was printed.

Quick note: certain aspects of property management differ between England, Scotland and Wales. In this section I cover what's applicable in England, so if your property is in Scotland or Wales you should check to see what differs locally.

Before marketing a property to let

- Get any consents you need, such as from your mortgage lender (if you're using a residential mortgage) and freeholder (check your lease to see what your obligations are).

- Obtain an **Energy Performance Certificate (EPC)** – which is legally required before you can market a property. These last for ten years and you can search **epcregister.com** to see if the property already has one.

Pre-tenancy

- Conduct thorough reference checks.

- Check that the tenant has the right to reside in the UK (see **gov.uk/check-tenant-right-to-rent-documents**).

- Register the deposit with an approved government scheme within 30 days of receiving it (see **gov.uk/tenancy-deposit-protection/overview**).

- Issue the tenant with the "prescribed information" provided by the tenancy deposit scheme within 30 days of receiving the deposit.

- Issue the latest version of the government's "How To Rent" leaflet (**gov.uk/government/publications/how-to-rent**).

- Draw up a tenancy agreement and get the tenant to sign it (see **gov.uk/tenancy-agreements-a-guide-for-land-lords/tenancy-types**).

- If the property has a gas supply, make sure the last gas safety certificate was issued within the last year and give a copy to the tenant.

- Make sure an electrical safety check has been carried out within the last five years, give a copy to the tenant, and conduct a visual check of the electrical installation.

- Draw up a thorough inventory with date-stamped photographs, and give the tenant seven days to request any amendments.

- Check that smoke detectors and carbon monoxide detectors are working on the first day of the tenancy.

- Inform the utility suppliers of the change of occupant and supply them with opening readings.

- Inform the local authority's council tax department of the change of occupant.

During the tenancy

- Inspect the condition of the property regularly.

- Check the smoke detectors and carbon monoxide detectors on every visit.

- Chase up any late rent payments immediately.

- Respond promptly to any notifications of repairs that are needed.

- Renew the gas safety certificate annually.

- At the end of a fixed term, negotiate a rent increase if justified (see gov.uk/private-renting/rent-increases).

- At the end of a fixed term, decide whether to leave the tenancy "rolling" or ask the tenant to commit to another fixed period.

Ending the tenancy

- Issue a Section 21 notice two months before you require possession of the property, which can't be any earlier than the end of a fixed term (see **gov.uk/evicting-tenants/section-21-and-section-8-notices**). Again, note that plans are afoot to remove Section 21 – so make sure you check and comply with whatever process is in place at the time.

- Check the tenant out by comparing the condition of the property to its condition in the opening inventory – ideally with the tenant present.

- Make sure all sets of keys are returned.

- Agree any deductions from the deposit with the tenant. If you can't reach an agreement, apply to the deposit scheme for dispute resolution.

- Release the balance of the deposit within ten days of deductions being agreed.

Extra protections

As a landlord you'll need buildings insurance (unless it's included as part of your service charge), and you might optionally decide to insure your contents if you let the property furnished. On top of these, there are extra policies you can take out to smooth out the bumps of property ownership.

One such policy, which has become increasingly popular over the last few years, is rent guarantee insurance (RGI). As the name suggests, it's a way of guaranteeing your income stream: if the tenant stops paying the rent, the insurance will kick in and make monthly payments to you. It will continue until the tenant either gets back on track or leaves, and some policies also cover the legal costs of the eviction process.

In principle, I'm a fan. Some people argue that insurers will only take on "safe bets" in the first place (they insist that the tenant passes their referencing process), and note that the insurance company needs to build in a margin so in the long run you'd be better off without. This is all entirely true, but I'd far rather come off worse in cash terms in exchange for having the worry of non-payment completely removed. Taking out RGI also means you can afford to hold a smaller reserve fund: rather than potentially having to meet eight months of expenses with no income (a nightmarish but entirely possible amount of time to evict a non-paying tenant) the insurer will pay you and you can use that money to pay the bills.

In practice though, RGI policies often come with a giant list of caveats, exceptions and excesses. They often won't take effect until payments are a month in arrears, might then take another month's payment as an "excess", and sometimes expect the deposit to be used to cover the missing rent before they start paying.

Start by searching for "rent guarantee insurance" and you'll be inundated with options. Don't just go for the cheapest: read the terms in detail to check what's covered, and make sure you're happy with the peace of mind you get for the price.

Another type of insurance of which I'm a definite fan is emergency cover. Policies vary, but this typically covers emergencies relating to heating, hot water, electricity, sanitation, security (external doors and windows) and pests. The idea is that you're given a 24-hour phone number to call in the event of an emergency, and someone will come out to resolve the situation free of charge.

As they'll only do whatever is necessary to stop the situation from being dangerous, it doesn't mean that you'll never need to pay for another repair again. But even if they're unable to permanently resolve the issue, by avoiding an emergency call-out charge and being able to arrange a proper repair later you'll save the year's premium at a stroke.

The other big advantage for self-managing landlords is that the 24-hour number can be given to your tenant, so if the boiler breaks down at 11pm, you won't get the call – the insurance provider will. All being well, you won't even find out about the problem until it's already been fixed.

I use Surewise (**surewise.com**) and have never had any problems with them, but if you search for "landlord emergency cover" you'll find lots of other options. Just bear in mind that, like with all insurance, they make it easy to buy and not always so easy to claim. Read the small print to find out what is and isn't covered – with boilers, for example, it often must be under a certain age and be serviced every year.

Chapter 13

Tax and accounting

Seldom has a chapter had a less prepossessing title, but please don't tune out: this chapter has the potential to save you more money than any other.

But still, bear in mind that I'm far from being an accountant and I'm not qualified to give financial advice. Anything to do with tax comes in lots of shades of grey (and not even the fun ones), so my only intention here is to explain the very basics and get you thinking about how tax might apply in your own situation. Before taking any action, you should read much more widely and take professional advice.

As this chapter goes on, you'll see why I didn't take tax into account for any of my scenarios in Part 1. Even though each property generates the same amount of income irrespective of who the owner is, the tax arising from that income will be totally different for an individual compared to a company, could be different for the *same* individual over time if they've built up a loss elsewhere or if it tips them into a different tax bracket, and can be affected again by whether the property is split between a married couple who have different levels of earnings.

We'll start with the very basics of record keeping and your obligations to the tax man. Then we'll take what *seems* like a detour into a very specific aspect of property taxation – but it actually sets the stage for the discussion of a common question: "Should I invest in my own name or through a limited company?"

After that we'll get into the expenses you can offset against tax, then put together everything we've covered to see how you can end up with a lower tax bill than you might have suspected. Psyched? I knew you would be!

Obligations and basics

Once you've bought a property in your own name, it's your responsibility to tell HMRC that they now have another method by which they can gouge money out of you. They've got no way of automatically knowing, which is great until they catch up with you a few years later and take action against you for tax evasion.

If you already fill in a tax return, all you need to do is fill in an extra page for your new property income. But if you're currently taxed via your employer, you need to notify HMRC of your need to complete a tax return. The easiest way is to call them using the details on their website.

Filling in that tax return used to be pretty straightforward: take the rental income, deduct all the allowable costs you incurred (which we'll come to), and whatever's left over is your profit. That profit is split between any joint owners, and it's added to your other sources of income when calculating the tax you owe. Now, as a result of the changes to the treatment of mortgage interest that took effect in April 2017, it's a bit more complicated – as we'll see in the next section.

Alternatively, if you buy a property within a company rather than in your own name, that company will need to file accounts. Then, when you draw profits out of the company, you'll be in exactly the same position as above: you'll either declare that income on your tax return if you already complete one, or let HMRC know that you now need to.

In terms of record keeping, everything becomes a lot easier if you have a separate bank account that's used solely for property transactions. Any normal current account will do: just have the rent as the only payment coming in, and expenses going out as direct debits or charged to the associated debit card. If you have a linked savings account, you can also get in the habit of regularly transferring funds across to cover tax and/or serve as a contingency fund. Whether you do the bookkeeping yourself or let your accountant handle it, it's a lot easier when the transactions are separated rather than intermingled with your own finances.

Speaking of which, do you need an accountant? When you're just starting out, not necessarily: if the sums are small, an accountant might not be able to save you more than they're costing you (as long as you get yourself clued up about what you can claim). Then again, getting the structure of your investments right from a tax perspective at the start is increasingly important, and much cheaper than trying to change things around later – so you might well consider it a worthwhile investment.

Property traders

If you're trading in property rather than investing, you get an easier ride through the rest of this chapter: you get to sit out the discussion on mortgage interest, the debate about whether to incorporate, and the distinction between "capital" versus "revenue" expenses.

What I mean by "trading" is that you're buying a property and selling it on again without renting it out in the meantime. In this scenario, you'll usually be better off buying within a company rather than as an individual (although be sure to check with an accountant first). Doing so means you'll pay corporation tax rather than income tax on your profits, which is significant for higher rate and additional rate taxpayers. Even basic rate taxpayers can come out ahead with a company through techniques like moving your "year end" date to minimise liabilities, which isn't possible for individuals. (An accountant can help with minimising any tax liabilities when extracting profits from a company, if you don't intend to let them build up within the company for future purchases.)

With corporate structure established, the accounting process of a property trader is straightforward: when you sell a property you can deduct all the costs you incurred along the way (everything from the finance arrangement fee at the start to the estate agent's fee at the end), and what's left over is subject to corporation tax.

That's not to say that there isn't more for traders to be aware of than is covered in this book. For now, I just want to give you enough information so that you can factor in the impact of tax on your trading business. Any further knowledge you gain from talking to an expert will have the potential to save you a lot of money.

What's the deal with mortgage interest?

In 2015, then-Chancellor George Osborne announced a major change to the way mortgage interest affects the tax affairs of property investors. It caused an almighty kerfuffle at the time, and even though it's now just part of investing life it's worth spending some time on – because it's different from how tax works in any other area of business, and takes a bit of wrapping your brain around at first.

Before getting into the details, it's important to be clear that this only affects *individual* property investors: the treatment of property within companies is the same as it was before. That's why I'm talking about this first, and *then* getting into the debate about whether you should incorporate – because it has a major effect on everything that follows.

Previously, property investment income would be treated in the same way as any other business: rent comes in, expenses go out, profit is what remains – and that profit is taxed. If you took out a mortgage to acquire a buy-to-let property, the monthly interest payments were considered to be a cost of doing business – and therefore they were deducted along with all your other costs before calculating the profit that's left over.

To put that into numbers:

- £10,000 rental income

- £5,000 mortgage interest costs

- £1,000 other costs

- = £4,000 profit

That £4,000 profit would be subject to your normal rate of tax – currently 20% for a basic rate taxpayer (meaning a tax bill of £800) and 40% for a higher rate taxpayer (meaning a tax bill of £1,600).

Here's the change: since April 2020, *mortgage interest can no longer be deducted as a cost of doing business*. Instead of deducting it before arriving at your profit figure, you first calculate your profit and then claim a *basic rate allowance* (currently 20%) for your mortgage interest before calculating the tax due.

This becomes a lot clearer with the help of an example:

- £10,000 rental income

- [£5,000 mortgage interest costs – NOT DEDUCTED]

- £1,000 other costs

- = £9,000 profit

- Allowance to apply: 20% of £5,000 interest costs = £1,000

A 20% taxpayer would therefore owe £1,800 in tax on their profit (20% of £9,000), then claim the allowance of £1,000, leaving them with a final tax bill of £800. A 40% taxpayer would owe £3,600 in tax on their profit (40% of £9,000), then claim the allowance of £1,000, leaving them with a final tax bill of £2,600.

Two things happen as a result of this unusual treatment.

The basic rate taxpayer appears to end up paying the same amount, so let's first take the case of a higher rate taxpayer. Clearly they have a higher tax bill, which was exactly the point of introducing this new method. The intention was to "level the playing field" between owner-occupiers who can't offset their interest against tax and property investors who can, but to limit that effect to higher rate taxpayers (who I presume the government thinks can afford it).

Investors were unhappy about the principle of the change, because the financing costs associated with acquiring capital assets are an allowable expense for every other type of business. (And because the new method doesn't apply to properties owned within a company, it's also an allowable expense for participants in the *same* industry if they have a different corporate structure.) But worse than the principle is the reality that if a higher rate taxpayer is highly leveraged, they can end up paying more in tax than they make in profit.

For example:

- A property worth £200,000 with a mortgage of 80% of its value (£160,000) at an interest rate of 5%

- £12,000 rental income

- [£8,000 mortgage interest costs - NOT DEDUCTED]

- £1,500 other costs

- = £10,500 profit

- Allowance to apply: 20% of £8,000 interest costs = £1,600

So the amount of actual cash that the investor has in their pocket after paying all their expenses is £2,500 (£12,000 - £8,000 - £1,500). Previously this would have resulted in a tax bill of £1,000 (40% of £2,500) and a post-tax profit of £1,500.

But their tax bill is now calculated as 40% of £10,500 (£4,200), minus the £1,600 allowance. That leaves them with a tax bill of £2,600 – which means they're now making a £100 loss!

Bad news, then, for higher rate taxpayers. But did you catch the other thing that happened? Because profit is now calculated *before* interest is deducted or allowances are claimed, *everyone's* income now appears to be higher. That means that a lot of investors who were previously basic rate taxpayers are pulled into the higher bracket – even if their portfolio is barely profitable.

Chances are, you're now asking yourself a very good question: if the new method is worse and it only applies to individual investors, is it better to buy properties within the structure of a company?

Should you incorporate?

As this book is targeted at newcomers and I don't want to over-complicate matters, I'm only going to talk about how to structure the purchase of properties you buy *from now on*. To decide whether it's a good idea to move properties you *already* own into a company, you should speak to an accountant.

My stock answer to the question of whether you should incorporate used to be "Probably not, if you're investing rather than trading". Traders, as I explained earlier, are usually better off buying within a company. As an investor though, it often wasn't worth it. Although you paid corporation tax at 19% rather than income tax at up to 45%, there were equivalent disadvantages (which we'll come to shortly), which balanced things out.

But The Great Tax Shock Of 2015 changed all that, and there are now two big advantages to investing through a company:

- You swerve the new treatment of mortgage interest, allowing you to deduct it in full before calculating your profit. (Although, note of caution: *for now*. In principle there's nothing to stop the government changing the rules to catch companies in the future too.)

- Your profits are subject to corporation tax rather than income tax, which will make a significant difference if you're a higher rate taxpayer.

So far, so good. But there are drawbacks too:

- If you want to draw profits out of the company to spend, you'll do so in the form of dividends and be taxed for doing so – meaning that as a higher rate taxpayer you could end up no further ahead than if you'd just bought in your own name and paid income tax.

  For example, a £1,000 profit taxed at an income tax rate of 40% leaves you with £600. A £1,000 profit taxed at a corporation tax rate of 19% leaves you with £810 – but you then pay a dividend tax rate of 32.5% (after the first £2,000 of dividends, which are tax-free) when you want to access the £810, leaving you with £546.75. So in this scenario, assuming you've used your dividend allowance, you end up worse off than you would have been by just paying income tax in the first place.

- If you've been renting out a property for a while and then choose to sell it, as an individual you can use your annual capital gains tax (CGT) allowance so you're not taxed on the full amount of the gain. A company doesn't get an allowance because gains are taxed as profit, so would likely end up paying more tax than an individual when selling the property.

Another disadvantage – although one that has improved markedly over the last few years – is that the number of lenders willing to lend to companies is more limited than it is for individuals. This tends to mean higher interest rates, lower loan-to-value ratios and higher arrangement fees. Even so, you might end up with a mortgage that's a bit more expensive but end up saving a lot of tax as a result – so you need to run your own personal numbers.

Because dramatically more investors have started using corporate vehicles over the last few years, lenders have responded accordingly and introduced more products with improved rates. This is only going to continue – so a good mortgage adviser to guide you through the options will be, as always, your best friend.

So should you incorporate? As a very general rule of thumb (which definitely doesn't constitute tax advice), investors tend to find it advantageous to buy within a company if they plan to leave the profits to build up within the company for future purchases until (for example) they quit full-time work and their tax position changes. If they plan to withdraw the profits as personal income, it's far more of a toss-up and it could well be better *not* to incorporate.

Again, I remind you that this is nothing more than a brief summary from a non-expert: weighing up the pros and cons and applying them to your own present situation and long-term goals is no easy matter. The right decision will depend on your current earnings, what you plan to do with the profits, what the future tax position of your portfolio is likely to be, whether you'll be selling properties, how much leverage you use, and many, many other factors.

In short, it's something you should take professional advice about rather than rely solely on a book. If this all sounds scary enough to put you off investing altogether, do reserve judgement until you've read the section on losses and tax planning in a moment – because the situation might not be as grim as it first appears.

Allowable expenses

If you've been glassily turning the pages through this section while your mind drifts off to the football or the Great British Bake Off, COME BACK! We've very nearly finished talking about tax, but it's really important that we cover this next section before we can move on to something more exciting (which is pretty much almost anything).

In the course of running your property business you'll incur expenses, and many of those expenses can be deducted from your income before arriving at your profit. The name of the game, then, is to make sure you claim every expense that you legitimately can: if you're paying tax on your profits at a rate of 40%, remembering to claim an extra £100 in expenses will reduce your tax bill by £40. Clearly it makes no sense to incur expenses for the sake of it, but you should get the most out of the expenses you can't avoid… and even be a bit strategic about it to extract maximum benefit.

Expenses fall into two different categories: *capital* expenditure, and *revenue* expenditure.

Capital expenditure relates to the costs of acquiring assets (in our case, that means properties), and costs relating to anything you do with that asset to materially increase its value. Examples would include:

- The actual purchase price of the property.

- Your legal fees for arranging the purchase.

- Any refurbishment work you do to a property *to make it lettable in the first place* (this becomes important in the next section).

- Any work you do to the property that improves it – and thus could increase its value. For example, converting the loft or adding an en suite bathroom.

Capital expenditure can't be deducted from your profits in the year in which you incur the expense. Instead, you can only reclaim these costs when you eventually *sell* the property.

For example, if you buy a property for £100,000, pay £2,000 in legal fees and immediately spend £50,000 refurbishing it, that's £152,000 in capital expenditure. If you sell the property for £300,000 in the future, you can deduct that £152,000 before calculating the CGT you will owe.

Expenses categorised as "capital" are no fun. You're shelling out now and getting nothing back for potentially decades – and by the time you can reclaim them, inflation means that the relief you're getting will be worth less to you than you paid out in the first place.

Everything that doesn't fall under the category of capital expenditure is automatically revenue expenditure instead. Revenue expenditure is much more like it: you incur a cost today, and can immediately offset it against your income. Examples include:

- Any fees you're charged by a letting agent.

- Any bills you pay as part of the rent.

- Any repairs you need to make to the property.

- Any furniture you buy for the property.

- Any refurbishment you do that broadly just *restores the property to its previous condition* rather than makes an improvement. For example, redecorating, or replacing a dated bathroom suite with a new one that looks more modern but isn't "better" in terms of its facilities.

In addition to these pretty obvious revenue expenses relating to specific properties, there's a range of more general expenses that also fall under the "revenue" category:

- Any relevant costs you incur for *seven years* prior to your property business starting – which could be tax advice, travel, business cards or anything else you can think of. Unfortunately, however, you can't make any claims relating to aborted transactions – so if you got a survey done on a property that subsequently fell through, that's not allowable.

- Any mileage you use in the course of property activities, which can be claimed at standard HMRC business rates.

- The costs of education, as long as it's classed as improving an existing skill rather than acquiring a new one. There's no clear guide as to where the dividing line between acquisition and improvement is, but you could argue that once you've read this book and gone on a cheap or free course, you've acquired the skill of property investment – so if you subsequently go on a £500 course, that could be claimed.

- Sustenance costs while running your business, within reason – so keep your receipts for the odd sandwich and coffee while you're out viewing properties.

- Postage costs, such as sending documents to solicitors.

- Telephone costs.

- If you run your business from home, you can claim an allowance for using your home as an office.

And more. As with everything in tax, there are grey areas aplenty here – which is why it's worth paying an accountant once you get to a certain point. If you're just starting out, no number of receipts for stamps and sandwiches will save you as much as an accountant charges, but when you get to a certain level it can give you the confidence to claim expenses that you weren't sure about or possibly weren't even aware of.

Losses and tax planning

The wonderful thing about tax (now there's a phrase I never thought I'd type) is that losses can be carried forward for as long as your business exists, until they're "wiped out" by equivalent profits.

To give an example, say you buy a property in Year 1 and in the process you pay your broker's fees and buy some white goods for the kitchen, then go on a full-day course (all classified as revenue expenses) – for a total spend of £3,000 before any rent comes in. That loss of £3,000 is carried forward to Year 2, during which you make a profit of £2,000. That means you still have an overall loss of £1,000 to carry forward to Year 3, which is the point at which you're first on track to become profitable and have tax to pay.

It's important to realise that profits and losses are calculated across your portfolio as a whole – so in any given year if you incur a whole load of costs on one particular property (as long as they're classified as "revenue" in nature), these costs will reduce or eliminate the profit you would otherwise have made on the rest of your portfolio. However, you can't offset property losses against *other* sources of income – your property portfolio is effectively a separate "business" in itself, even if you own the properties in your own name.

(This is another reason why it doesn't make sense to look at the projected returns from a property and say "Oh but that doesn't take tax into account", and it's why I didn't include tax in my explanations of strategies in Part 1. The tax that's payable is determined by the portfolio as a whole, so you can't factor it into a discussion of one particular property.)

Once you appreciate these facts (that the profits/losses that determine tax liability are calculated across the whole portfolio, and losses can be carried forward), you start to see that while you're in the acquisition phase, it's possible to structure your affairs to pay less tax than you might think.

Let's see how. Say you buy a property that's fundamentally sound but somewhat dated internally, and it comes with a tenant already in situ. Six months later, the tenant gives notice and you take the opportunity to refurbish the property before you move the next tenant in – costing £7,000.

As we saw in the last section, restoring a property to its previous condition rather than making improvements can be classified as a "revenue" expense. This is the case even if you do the refurbishment before letting the property out for the first time. (Although you'd be wise to keep records showing that you would have been able to rent the property out even if you'd chosen not to do the works – otherwise HMRC might push for it to be counted as a "capital" expense.) In the current example, though, you'd already rented the property out for six months so it's not an issue.

Let's say the refurbishment consisted of replacing single-glazed windows with double glazing (not considered an improvement, because putting in single glazing nowadays isn't an option), replacing a grotty old bathroom suite (an improvement aesthetically but not functionally, which is critical) and giving the whole place new carpets and a lick of paint. Those changes might allow you to increase the rent, and might even increase the value of the property if you ever wanted to refinance or sell it on – but nevertheless, they're "revenue" in nature.

That £7,000 spend might eliminate the profit from the rest of your portfolio, or even give you a loss to carry forward. So if you're in acquisition mode and buying one such property per year, you may not have tax to worry about for quite a while.

To take it a step further, let's say that a couple of years later you sell the property for £10,000 more than you paid for it as a result of the refurbishment. This £10,000 profit will count as a *capital gain* – and if you bought the property in your own name, this will fall within your annual allowance so there'll be no tax to pay.

It's easier to follow if we put in some made-up numbers:

- Year 1: £500 rental profit (£200 tax to pay, assuming a 40% rate of income tax)

- Year 2: £1,000 rental profit, £7,000 refurbishment cost (no tax to pay, £6,000 loss carried forward)

- Year 3: £1,000 rental profit (still £5,000 loss to carry forward)

- Year 4: £1,000 rental profit (still £4,000 loss to carry forward)

- Year 5: Property sold for £10,000 more than the purchase price (capital gain within allowance, still £4,000 loss to carry forward)

Forgetting the capital/revenue distinction and putting it in "real life" terms, you've walked away £3,000 better off after paying for the refurbishment (you made £10,000 and the refurbishment cost you £7,000), paid no tax on your rental income for four years and still ended up with a loss to offset your tax in future years.

There are important subtleties in here. For a start, you'd need to make sure that your expenses were *genuinely* revenue in nature – and if the refurbishment included an element of capital improvement too, you should try to get any tradespeople to separate out their invoices to keep it neat. For example, if the same company added a loft conversion (improvement, hence capital) and repainted all the existing internal walls (reinstatement, hence revenue) you should ask them to issue a separate invoice for each job. Secondly, enough time needs to elapse for you not to be "gaming the system": there are no hard and fast rules, but if you bought a property, let it out for a month, refurbished it, let it for another few months and sold it, eyebrows might be raised at HMRC. Or they might not – such is the nature of grey areas – but the eyebrow raise might happen after you've done the same thing for the fourth time in two years.

In short, I'm saying that by understanding the basics of how property profits are taxed, you can optimise your activities to keep your tax bill down – especially while you're in the acquisition phase. You can see how, timed correctly, you could avoid making a paper profit for years – perhaps until your income from other sources (such as employment) has dropped off and put you into a lower tax bracket, for example.

But I'll say it one last time: *this is not a tax book*. I want to give you enough knowledge to get you thinking about what's possible, but please, make sure this is the start of your education process rather than the end. Take professional advice rather than rely on what you read in this book or online, and make sure you're not knowingly or unknowingly breaking any rules or storing up unintended consequences.

It may be tempting to stretch the rules and sail close to the wind, but it's not worth the stress. While an investigation is unlikely to happen, I prefer to make sure I could sit across the table from an HMRC representative and confidently explain my tax arrangements without any concern.

Chapter 14

Selling

Whether you've held a property for a couple of weeks or a couple of decades, the day may come when it's time to bid it a tearful goodbye, delete it from your portfolio spreadsheet, and start planning for what you're going to do with the cash you raise from the sale.

Much of what you need to know about selling a property has already been covered: all the considerations are the same as when you're buying, but you're on the other side of the transaction. There are some elements we haven't yet discussed though, so in this chapter we'll look at how to sell (for top dollar) a property you're flipping, how to decide whether to sell a buy-to-let property, and how to survive the legal process in either case.

Achieving the best price when buying to sell

It's wildly obvious to say that you only make your money on a flip once you sell, but it's something that amateur investors often seem to forget: instead, they get all excited about buying it and finding ways to express their creativity while doing it up.

The most successful property traders, meanwhile, are thinking about the sale from the very beginning – *while they're still deciding what to buy* – and they see everything else as just steps they have to go through before they can put it on the market.

From the moment you start looking at areas and properties, you need to be thinking about the sale at the end. We covered this earlier, but if you buy in an area where there isn't much owner-occupier demand, you've already put yourself at a giant disadvantage. Conversely, if you buy somewhere with considerable demand and not much supply, any mistakes you make will affect you less severely.

When you're planning your refurbishment, every pound you spend should be targeted at improvements that will induce a potential buyer to pay more at the end. For this reason, I'd recommend getting an estate agent around to see the project and offer advice as early as possible, because they see a lot of houses and hear the comments that hundreds of potential buyers make. Should you knock through a wall to make an open-plan living area? Should you put in an en suite or an extra downstairs bathroom? I don't know, you don't know, but an estate agent will.

Whatever your refurb budget, I strongly recommend setting aside some money for professional photos. It makes no sense to me when people sink six figures into a project and then baulk at spending £100 on a decent set of photos – preferring instead to let the agent's dodgy iPhone snaps represent all the hard work they've put in. Selling the property involves getting people through the door, which relies on them spotting the property on the portals or in the estate agent's window, which in turn relies on your property standing out from all the other listings so that they'll pick up the phone and book a viewing. There's no doubt that professional photos make a property stand out: just browse Rightmove yourself (always a fun distraction) and notice that it's the ones with clear, bright pictures that get your click.

Another highly worthwhile thing to consider (but admittedly more pricey than photos) is staging the property with furniture. *You* might be able to look at the blank canvas and visualise what it will look like when beautifully furnished, but not everyone can. Your aim is to find the buyer who walks through the door, pictures themselves living there, and will be willing to pay any price because they can't bear to lose it. And if that buyer needs to see it nicely staged to make that happen, you'll have lost the sale if you were too cheap/lazy to put in the effort.

You can either buy furniture and move it from house to house (if you're planning on undertaking multiple projects), or rent it on a month-by-month basis. Either way, it's going to cost you more than you want it to – but if it tempts one extra buyer into a bidding war that adds £10,000 to the final selling price, that's one heck of a return on investment. This is one area where effort is rewarded: the most successful property trader I know has a lock-up garage full of cushions and homely little touches, which get moved from house to house. It's a lot of work, but everything up to this point has been a lot of work so it seems a shame to stop now.

Once everything is beautifully staged, the next step in making the sale is to price it correctly. Buyers may be emotion-driven, but they're not daft: an overpriced property will receive fewer viewings, and the viewings that *do* happen will be less likely to convert into offers because they were expecting something truly spectacular for the price.

My personal preference is to price very slightly below what other similar properties are going for. If an un-staged property with amateur photos has an asking price of £160,000, my beautifully presented property at £155,000 is going to stand out a mile. I'll get more viewings – and that will lead to quick offers, competition, and fear of missing out. Worst case, I'll get a quick sale – which will allow me to bank the profit and move on to the next project. Best case, the large number of viewings will spark a bidding war and it'll end up selling for far more than the asking price.

Of course, you can only price it right if you gave yourself enough room in your figures: if you buy at too high a price and spend too much, you could easily end up needing to sell at an astronomical figure just to break even. That's why it's so important to think about the sale before you even buy.

If you've ticked all the boxes – bought in the right area, got the spec right, presented it attractively and priced it well – then you should find the offers coming in thick and fast. Accepting the offer isn't, sadly, the end of the story – there are still hurdles to overcome during the legal process. The issues you'll face are the same for flips as they are for buy-to-lets, so we'll consider both together later in this chapter.

Why sell a BTL?

Well, why would you? After all, properties always go up in value in the long run. Once you start talking to people about property investment, you'll soon get sick of hearing about how they'd be a millionaire by now if they hadn't sold that Notting Hill flat in the 1980s. Add to that the capital gains tax bill when you sell, *plus* the lost income that the property was generating for you, and selling doesn't look like a particularly attractive option.

The logic is sound, and investors generally prefer to expand their portfolios by *refinancing* to access equity (which we'll cover in more detail in Part 3) rather than selling. In reality though, there are several situations in which you might want to sell a property.

Firstly, and simply enough, not every property you buy is going to be an absolute slam-dunk of a success – especially at the start of your investment career. You might have invested in a house that you thought would be a superstar, but it's actually a B-league player at best (or is even losing you money); it makes more sense to offload it and use the funds to buy better next time. There will be points in time that are particularly favourable to shifting under-performing properties (which we'll look at far more in Part 3), and it can be wise to seize those opportunities.

Or maybe you've given your strategy some thought and realised you hold properties that aren't aligned with your goals (for example, you might own high-yielding properties when what you're really after is capital growth). That being the case, you might decide to sell what you've got and buy something else.

Or you might detect that a property has already done what you wanted and no longer serves a purpose for you. Perhaps you bought it when the local market was depressed and it's risen in value nicely since you bought it, but it doesn't yield brilliantly and seems to have given you all the growth you're going to get. Again, you might decide to sell and look for opportunities elsewhere.

In every case, the argument for selling emerges when you recognise that the *opportunity cost* of holding the property is too high: if you were to sell, your money could be put to better use elsewhere.

That's not to say that you *must* sell in these situations – you might be very happy with the returns you're getting, even if it's possible you could get higher returns elsewhere. What matters is to judge each situation on its merits, related to your strategy – not to just accept the "never sell" mantra at face value.

Should you sell with the tenant in situ?

If you do decide to sell a buy-to-let property, you'll have a dilemma to contend with: do you sell it with vacant possession, or with tenants in situ?

In the past, vacant possession has been the way to go, and it may still be. By selling the property tenanted, you're excluding the biggest part of the market – people who are buying a property to live in – and appealing only to investors, who (especially if they've read this book) aren't going to be inclined to give you your full asking price because they've just "got a feeling that this is the one". You also won't be able to present the property as well as you could do if it were empty, and you might even struggle to get access for viewings if the tenants choose to be difficult about it.

All that said, a big drawback of selling a vacant property is that you'll be losing out on income while it sits empty. It could easily take a few months to accept an offer, followed by another couple of months for the legal gears to grind along. And during this time without rental income coming in, you've got mortgage payments to meet, higher insurance payments (because it's empty), and council tax to pay (unless your local authority offers an exemption for empty properties).

For those reasons, you might prefer to sell the property with tenants in place. This is becoming increasingly popular, because the proportion of investors (rather than owner-occupiers) in the market has increased in recent years. For investment buyers, a tenanted property is a bonus: they'll have income from day one, and won't have to spend money on marketing or refurbishing.

So which option should you choose? It depends on the property itself, as well as the local market. If local estate agents tell you that the majority of people who've bought similar properties recently have been investors, marketing it as "tenanted" could be the answer. Conversely, if it's a family home in a popular area, you'd be doing yourself a major disservice by excluding the owner-occupier market – the financial hit you'll take from it being empty while it's up for sale should be more than compensated for by the higher price you'll eventually receive.

The sales process

If you're feeling nostalgic for the boring, drawn-out and stressful legal process you experienced when you were buying the property, I have good news for you: you get to do it all again when you sell. You're on the other side of the deal of course, but you'll still be able to get involved in all manner of cajoling (ah, the memories!), and you're still bound to have at least one sleepless night when you're convinced that it's all going to fall through.

There are a few extra decisions you get to make as the vendor, though.

Firstly, you get to set the asking price. Just like when you're trying to assess the value of a property you want to buy, you should set your selling price by looking at similar, nearby properties that have sold recently. From there you can add a cheeky premium if you're feeling confident, or go in low if you need to shift it quickly.

You'll also need to decide *how* to sell it: should you use an estate agent, act as estate agent yourself, or sell at auction?

In a post-Homes Under The Hammer world, selling at auction isn't a bad idea. Auctions were once the hunting ground of specialist buyers or builders looking for a new project, but are now seen as "somewhere to grab a bargain" by the general buying public. (As one investor put it, he stopped buying at auction and started selling there instead once all the white vans in the car park had been replaced by family cars.)

As a result, properties can end up being sold at auction for more than they'd fetch through an estate agent – with the added bonus that the legal process only takes 28 days, so you won't be stuck with an empty property for months on end. There's luck involved on the day of course, but it's worth considering.

If you decide to stay away from auctions, the next decision is whether to use an estate agent or play the agent yourself. In a hot market, there's a strong case for doing it yourself: all an agent will do is stick the listing online and wait for the phone to ring, so you could save money by advertising it on the online portals directly and taking care of the viewings. Just bear in mind that if it takes you an extra few weeks to sell (compared to how quickly an agent could shift it), your gains could be wiped out by the extra holding costs you'll incur. The same applies for any extra time taken as a result of not having an agent playing Chief Nag in the dance of the solicitors.

And then, of course, your final decision is which offer to accept. How far should you push a buyer? Should you favour a slightly lower cash offer over a higher bidder who's relying on a mortgage? It's up to you, but one thing's for sure: the person who's most desperate for the deal to happen will come off worst. So put yourself in a position of strength by doing everything you need to do to attract plenty of bids. Make the property easy for someone to fall irrationally in love with, and you can't go too far wrong.

PART 3:
BUILDING A LONG-TERM PORTFOLIO

Introduction

By the time you've followed all the steps in Part 2, you'll have made your first transaction. Whether you're holding it for the long haul or you've sold it on again for a profit, you can officially call yourself A Property Investor. Congratulations!

While your first investment experience no doubt caused you a fair amount of stress and fear, there's a good chance you're now hooked. As soon as the first month's rent drops into your bank account or the proceeds of the sale are transferred over by your solicitor, all the boredom, frustration and confusion you've experienced get forgotten – and you just want to do it all again.

Which is just as well – because as we saw in Part 1, making a *real* difference to your financial life involves doing far more than just buying one property.

Knowing how to buy an individual property (and buy it well) is a necessary component of successful property investing, but on its own it isn't enough: even the best purchase won't allow you to retire, quit your job or whatever your goal is.

So you'll need to expand your portfolio, making effective use of the cash, equity and skills at your disposal. You'll need to understand the property cycle so that you can *time* your buying and selling activity correctly – which is probably the most important factor that most amateur investors don't have a clue about. You'll need to execute your strategy successfully through all the ups and downs of the market, using downturns as a golden buying opportunity rather than a reason to be fearful. And eventually, the time will come when your goal has been achieved and it's time to think about an exit strategy.

No book could call itself "complete" without covering these topics, so strap yourself in for Part 3 – where we'll take you from being "someone who's bought a property" to having the mind-set of a strategic, long-term property investor who's prepared for enduring and large-scale success.

Chapter 15

Financing portfolio growth

If you ask most investors what their current barriers to growth are, they'll say "access to finance". And while raising funds for deposits is undoubtedly a major challenge, I feel like it *should* be that way: nobody has an inherent right to collect large numbers of houses, and there's no reason why banks should lend money if you're not putting anything into the deal yourself. We had a brief, anomalous period of history where anyone could shovel up large numbers of properties without putting any cash into the deal, and that didn't end particularly brilliantly.

So, rightly in my view, if you want to buy multiple properties you'll need to put the effort into raising the finance. Broadly speaking, there are five ways of making this happen:

1.   Socking in more of your own cash

2.   Creating equity that can be accessed

3.   Waiting for the market to create equity for you

4.   Raising funds with a parallel strategy

5.   Bringing in outside finance

As we go through, you'll notice that some of these financing techniques were the basis of the strategies we saw all the way back in Part 1.

Option 1: Putting in more cash

It's simple and it's effective, and we saw this option in action back in the first strategy of Part 1. If you're able to save up enough money from other endeavours to consistently fund deposits, then you don't have much to worry about – and as you start re-investing rental profits too, you start a "snowball" effect that allows you to put in progressively less of your other savings over time. Every property you buy gives you more monthly profit, and your percentage of debt against equity reduces over time because your borrowing stays static while the value of the property increases.

There are really no downsides to this approach. If you're able to save up (say) £20,000 each year to use as a deposit, you're winning at life. If you're able to save up enough to buy a property wholly in cash each year, then you're *really* winning at life and you should just post me my First Class tickets to your private island so we can talk through the rest of the book in person.

Well, I said there were no downsides, but you *could* consider a downside to be that you're not getting as much bang for your buck as you would if you pursued a more sophisticated strategy. For example, if you were able to save up £20,000 each year *and* propel your portfolio growth by buying below market value and refinancing, you could use that extra £20,000 to either buy even more properties or invest in a totally different asset class.

This is true, but there's no law that says you *have* to maximise everything all the time. It all comes back to having a meaningful goal in mind before you start: if two people have the same goal but one of them has a lot more cash they can invest in achieving it, the person with more cash won't have to work as hard or accept as much risk to get to the same place.

Option 2: Creating equity

This is the refinancing (or "recycling") strategy we saw in Part 1. By buying at a great price and/or adding value, you're effectively creating equity out of thin air – which you can tap into to invest in further properties.

A quick recap: let's say you buy a property for £100,000 using a deposit of £25,000 and a mortgage for £75,000 (75% loan-to-value). If you subsequently manage to get the property revalued at £135,000, you can refinance to 75% of its new value and borrow £101,250. You pay back the £75,000 you borrowed at the start, and you've got your original deposit back to use again.

However, we also discussed earlier that even though your loan-to-value remains the same, your monthly interest payment goes up: at an interest rate of 5%, your monthly interest payment would have jumped from £312.50 to £421.87.

As a result, this strategy only works with properties that yield relatively well in the first place. If the property in our example only brought in £400 per month in rent (a 4.8% yield), you might *just about* break even after other costs with mortgage payments of £312.50 – but you wouldn't be able to refinance and increase your payments to £421.87 because you'd be losing money every month. If the property brought in £600 per month (a 7.2% yield), you'd have no such problem.

As long as you're buying properties that yield highly enough, this is a pretty great strategy: you're creating equity that didn't exist and using that equity (instead of your own cash) to fund your next deposit.

It doesn't particularly matter whether you create that equity by buying at a great price or by adding value. Indeed, the most common situation is for there to be a bit of both: a property that needs some work (potential to add value) will languish on the market because nobody wants to take on the task, and as a result you can buy it for a bargain price.

One thing to keep in mind for planning purposes is the timescale in which you can tap into this extra equity. As a rule (although there are exceptions), you'll need to own a property for at least six months before you can refinance at a higher level – and once that time comes, you'll need to produce evidence for the value you've added to justify a higher valuation. If you *haven't* added any value and just bought at a great price, a mortgage company will be reluctant to give you a higher valuation so quickly – and you might need to wait a couple of years before the full value can be realised.

It's also worth bearing in mind that this approach becomes less attractive if you're a higher rate taxpayer buying properties in your own name, because increasing your mortgage balance will have an unpleasant effect on your tax bill. You'll need to factor this into your calculations to make sure you're still making a post-tax profit after refinancing.

Nevertheless, however you create the equity cushion, in theory it allows you to have enough money for just one deposit and "recycle" those funds infinitely by pulling all your cash back out to use again. In practice, it's *very* difficult to get all of your cash back out – but even if you can get half of it out, that doubles the speed at which you can grow your portfolio compared to saving up a whole new deposit each time.

Option 3: Waiting for the market to rise

I'm no military strategist (which shouldn't come as a shock), but I doubt any great battles have been won through a strategy of "waiting and hoping". Sure, property prices generally increase over time – but if that's what you're relying on to release equity, you effectively have no control over how fast you go.

As long as you're in no mad rush and can fund any further acquisitions with more cash in the meantime, buying properties with an eye on medium-term capital growth is a perfectly valid thing to do. Doing so intelligently involves targeting the right type of property at the right time.

Consider the property first. All else being equal, a desirable property in a prime location will experience the strongest growth when the market is doing well. Buying such a property and waiting for growth doesn't give you a lot of control, but you have a better chance of success than if you buy a flat in an edge-of-town housing estate and do the same thing.

Then consider timing. There are times when house prices are going nuts, and other times when they're flat or falling. Clearly you don't want to be buying at the peak of the frenzy and risk the music stopping just as you complete, but equally you don't want to be buying at the start of a protracted period of flat prices if your strategy relies on refinancing or selling in the next couple of years. The same goes for selling: you absolutely don't want to be a forced seller when the market is struggling (the coming chapter on surviving a recession will protect you against this risk), but if you can see the market approaching its peak, you can offload properties and lock in your paper gains.

There's also the idea of "hotspots": you could buy in an area that's primed for explosive growth then just wait and hope, but that's a lot harder than you might think. Unless you're unusually skilled or have incredible local knowledge, I consider chasing hotspots to be a distraction. Whenever I've bought in a hotspot, it's been a total accident.

This is all tied into the idea of the property cycle, which we'll turn to in the next chapter. The message for now is that "wait and hope" is never an ideal strategy because you aren't in control, but it's possible to combine it intelligently with another approach. For example, use a primary strategy of just putting in more cash (Option 1) or buying properties where you can build in equity (Option 2), and also buy in such a way that the market is likely to give you an extra boost within the next few years.

Option 4: A parallel strategy

A common parallel to the buy-to-let strategy is buy-to-sell: make a profit from flipping a property, take that profit to use as the deposit on a buy-to-let, and put your original capital into your next buy-to-sell project.

Assuming that trading is something you're comfortable with and can execute successfully, this is an expansion strategy without many drawbacks. You're using the same skills and knowledge to both raise the capital and invest the capital, and if you can't exit a buy-to-sell deal for some reason, you can always temporarily add it to your buy-to-let portfolio.

Just like with Options 2 and 3, this strategy is best when combined with another source of funding too. If buy-to-sell projects are your only source of funding for your buy-to-let portfolio, you'll find yourself at a standstill if things don't go as planned.

For example, say your goal is to do two flips each year to make £30,000 post-tax profit, and then use that £30,000 as the deposit on one buy-to-let property. If in any given year one of your projects goes badly and you only end up breaking even, you can't add to your buy-to-let portfolio that year.

An alternative parallel strategy is to raise funds by selling opportunities to other investors. If you're able to find more attractive deals than your funds allow you to buy, you can always sell these deals on and take a "sourcing fee" – which goes towards your next deposit.

This isn't really any different from putting in more cash – it just happens to be cash that's raised from property endeavours rather than a day job – but it's worth mentioning all the same because it's a strategy that many investors employ very successfully.

Option 5: Joint ventures

If you don't have piles of spare cash lying around, plenty of other people will – and many of them will be happy to co-invest in property to make a better return than they'd get in a bank.

Joint venture deals can be structured in any way that suits both parties, but some of the most common are:

- The investor gets a fixed percentage return on the cash they put in (typically anything between 6% and 12% per year, but can be anything you negotiate).

- For buy-to-sell, one partner puts in the money and the other does the work. Profits are split at the end.

- For buy-to-let, both partners pool resources and co-own the property for years to come – splitting the costs and the rental income. (This is probably more suitable for family members, as it's a long-term shared financial commitment.)

Joint ventures can be a great solution for experienced investors who've exhausted their own cash or have it tied up in other projects. What I'm dubious about, though, is seeing joint ventures touted as a way to get started in property for someone who doesn't have access to cash for a deposit. I don't see why anyone would hand their cash over to someone without a demonstrable track record – and I don't think it's a good idea to make your mistakes and learn your lessons on someone else's dime. An exception to this would be taking money from family: it's still dangerous territory, but the motivations are easier to understand.

When it comes to structuring a joint venture – even with a close friend or family member – I *strongly* recommend drawing up a formal agreement stating:

- Who's putting what in

- Who will be performing which tasks

- What security each partner will have

- .What Plan A and Plan B for the project are

- What happens at the end if it concludes successfully

- What could go wrong, and what you will do in each situation

The last point is an important one, but it's often overlooked. It's fun to sit back and dream about how you'll spend your massive profits, but the wheels fall off joint venture agreements when things don't go to plan and the partners can't decide how they should be resolved. Thinking about this sort of thing in advance has two main advantages. Firstly, it makes sure you're on the same page about the project in general. And secondly, it means you can use the agreement as a "manual" about what should happen in any situation.

So joint ventures aren't something to rush into, and they definitely aren't a cure-all for cash-strapped investors. But the right partners could be a valuable alternative to banks once you've got your model locked down and want to expand.

Chapter 16

The property cycle

When I become a pub bore in my old age, I won't be droning on about Gloucestershire's batting averages or how much better everything was in the old days. No: I'll be on everyone's "avoid eye contact" lists because I won't stop talking about the property cycle.

Actually, I'm not far off that point already – but I have good reasons. Once you understand the property cycle, you'll know:

- That there's a reason *why* property prices always go up in the long run – giving you more confidence that they will continue to do so.

- That they *won't* go up in a nice smooth, straight line: crashes along the way are inevitable because of the way the system is set up. This allows you to prepare for them in advance (a subject so important I'm dedicating the next chapter to it).

- That you can ignore what the newspapers say about property prices, and have a far better understanding of what's likely to happen next by looking for certain signals in the world around you.

In short, a lot of facets of property investment that seem random or uncertain will suddenly make a lot more sense. With this knowledge you can at least avoid making the wrong move at the wrong time that would put your portfolio in jeopardy – and at most, you can make it a central pillar of your investment strategy.

Why is there a property cycle?

In pretty much every market other than land – whether it's goods like cars, or labour like hairdressers – the forces of supply and demand keep prices roughly in balance. If we all become more vain and start having our hair cut every day, it will be impossible to get an appointment and hairdressers will raise their prices to profit from those desperate enough to pay more for their coiffure. Soon, these higher prices will attract new hairdressers into the market, and the extra supply will mean that everyone has to reduce their prices to remain competitive. I'm not sure I'd want to have my hair cut by someone who'd only just entered the market because they saw how much money they could make, but that's by the by: the point is that supply and demand work in tandem to keep prices stable over time.

In the land market though, this can't happen because the amount of land in existence is fixed: you can't just magic up a load of extra land if demand for it goes up. (Yes, you could relax planning restrictions, but this is so politically fraught it doesn't usually happen. And in any case, demand is normally concentrated around established locations.) As a result, when the economy is growing and there's demand for new homes, shops and factories, that extra demand will push prices up. And because there's no supply mechanism to pull prices back down, land prices increase faster than wages and the price of goods. (For the geeks, this is related to Ricardo's Law of Rent, and it explains why rents account for an ever larger share of the economy over time. There's a simple explanation at **propertygeek.net/ricardo**.)

It doesn't take people long to realise what's happening and see that they'll get the best return on their money if they put it into property (as a proxy for land). At times of particularly high demand, people "speculate" by buying property on the assumption that the price will continue to go up.

Because property prices increase faster than wages do, property eventually becomes unaffordable for the majority of people. When this happens, the bust comes: property prices plummet, causing chaos for the banks (which have been lending money secured against high-priced property). The banks withdraw lending, building activity stops, and businesses shut down – which all have obvious knock-on effects for stock markets and employment levels.

Eventually of course, prices drop to a more sustainable level and everything gradually goes back to normal – at which point the whole cycle starts again. Importantly, each cycle starts from a higher "bottom" than the previous one – so the long-term trend is always upwards, even though there's a lot of volatility along the way.

That, in a nutshell, is the property cycle. It *would* be more accurate to call it "the land cycle", because the cost of building a house on a piece of land is much the same in London as it is in Leeds, and won't cost more in 100 years (other than inflation) than it does today. But house prices are more accessible to us than land prices, so we can "read" property prices to tell us what's happening in the land market – and therefore what's ahead for the wider economy.

The stages of the cycle

The economist Fred Harrison was one of the first people to identify the existence of the property cycle. He traced it back for hundreds of years to conclude that the length of a full cycle averages out to 18 years, with each cycle divided into distinct stages.

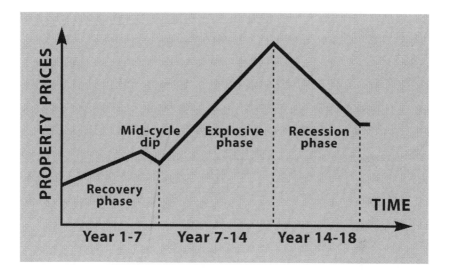

I'll argue later that the "18 year" part is a bit of a distraction, but understanding the characteristics of each stage is the key to recognising where we are in the cycle and taking action accordingly.

Unless you've picked up this book instead of Thomas The Tank Engine in some kind of terrible mix-up, you will have a memory of at least one complete property cycle – possibly more. As we talk about the indicators that signify each stage, you'll probably be able to think back to the clues that were there, in retrospect, in cycles you've experienced in the past.

This is critical because if you don't look for your own evidence, the media will lead you astray. After all, in 2006 did you see more headlines saying "Quick – you've got a year or two to sell everything!" or "How to get the best rates on 110% mortgages"? As we'll see, at every stage, the professionals who are watching the signals act *very* differently from the amateurs who are watching the media – and they get far better results.

So, let's take a look at each stage of the cycle, what drives the shift from one stage to the next, and what different types of investors are thinking and doing at each point...

We'll start as prices have bottomed out at the end of the recession, and the **recovery phase** is just beginning to get underway. Prices have fallen far enough to tempt the bravest investors back into the market, attracted by the high yields that are on offer as a result of prices falling while rents stay pretty much the same. (Rents don't fall because everyone still needs somewhere to live. Even if renters were brave enough to take advantage of the lower prices and buy, this is the toughest point in the cycle at which to get a mortgage because banks are struggling too.)

These brave investors are what we can think of as the "smart money": contrarian investors who've spotted the opportunity to get in at rock bottom, and are willing to take the risk of buying up assets while confidence is low and the investment case is still unproven. Of course, nobody knows precisely at what point the bottom of the market has been reached. Smart investors are just willing to take an educated guess, based on the knowledge that their upside potential is greater than their downside risk.

Meanwhile, amateur investors are totally absent from the market – even though lower prices and lack of competition mean that it's precisely the best time to buy. They might even crystallise their losses by selling at the bottom of the cycle "before prices fall any further", or be forced to sell because their portfolio was poorly structured to weather a recession. (We'll talk about how to survive a crash in the next chapter.)

So, if there's pessimism all around you and the media is full of doom and gloom even though the major catastrophic events of the recession seem to be over, the recovery phase might just be getting underway.

As the recovery phase develops, more buyers will have the confidence to enter the market – having the effect of pushing prices gradually upwards. Look out for big companies and pension funds starting to buy up distressed portfolios: they have the market intelligence to get in early but can't take the risk of getting in *too* early, so it's a good signal of the recovery solidifying. The prime assets will always be the most attractive, so this early growth tends to begin in the centres of the most economically powerful cities and "ripple out" from there.

Perhaps following a slight mid-cycle dip as the earliest movers take their profits, the recovery phase will give way to the **explosive phase**. It's now clear that prices are on the up, and the banks will be over the shock and willing to start lending again. That supplies enough confidence and capital for major building projects to start again, so expect to see more cranes on the skyline.

House prices will begin to increase markedly faster than wages, and it's at this point that the media gets interested – you'll probably start to see headlines along the lines of "House prices increasing by £200 a day" and "My house earned more than I did last month". Fuelled by this, people start to speculate: they either "move up the ladder" to somewhere bigger before it gets even further out of their reach, or they increase the mortgage against their home to fund holidays and cars. Banks make it easy for them to do so, because everything's in full swing and they just want to lend as much as they can.

At some point, logic and fundamentals go out the window and group psychology kicks in. The higher prices go, the more everyone assumes that prices will keep going up – so they buy at any level, pushing prices even further. The smart investors who got in early will be quietly selling off their holdings to lock in their profits, but the mania is such that nobody will notice.

As we move towards the peak of the explosive phase, it's a seller's market, and sellers know it – so estate agents conduct "open house"-style block viewings to stoke demand even further. Even properties that wouldn't have excited anyone a few years earlier end up going to sealed bids. Properties routinely sell for well above their asking price, and developers start marketing ever more "off plan" properties to capitalise on the demand.

Banks aren't immune to the mania, so they loosen their lending criteria to grab a bigger piece of the action. Even if some individuals within the banks are aware that the boom is unsustainable, they're still under pressure to compete with everyone else:

shareholders won't be happy with them sitting back and not lending while everyone else is so optimistic.

This lax credit keeps the party going for longer than anyone would previously have expected. At some point, a commentator or economist will predict that everything's about to come crashing down because everything is so fundamentally overvalued – but a year later prices will still be rising, and that commentator will be branded a "doom-monger".

The final couple of years of the explosive phase, as prices and mania reach their peak, are what Fred Harrison branded the **winner's curse phase**. Why's it a curse to be a "winner" by placing the highest bid for a property during this time? Because the next recession isn't far away, and it won't be long before the asset you've bought will be worth markedly less.

You obviously can't know when the "final years" of the upswing are until they've already happened and it's too late, but there's no shortage of warning signs that we may be near the top if you know where to look.

One such sign is the announcement of overblown building projects like "world's tallest building", "Europe's largest shopping centre", and other sorts of over-ambitious ideas. These projects are conceived at a time of supreme confidence and funded in a permissive lending environment. It's often the case that the bust has already happened by the time they're completed, and they sit mostly empty – a monument to the delusion that has just passed.

Another surefire sign is the rationalising of the ridiculously high prices that the mania has brought about. Justifications will be found for why "things are different this time" and we're in for an era of permanently higher prices... yet at some point reality will set in, and the **recession phase** is imminent.

Because the market was being driven by sentiment rather than fundamentals in the frothiest years, it's easy for confidence to suddenly evaporate and take the market with it. Prices plummet, and people who are over-leveraged go bankrupt – triggering waves of forced selling, which pushes prices down even further. It's impossible to pinpoint the exact moment when this is going to happen, but you won't need to be told when it does: nothing sells newspapers like bad news, so the media will stoke the panic with endless horror stories.

The recession phase seems like it will last forever, but it never does: at some point the smart money will be tempted back in, and the whole thing can start all over again.

How can we use the cycle?

So far in this chapter we've seen why property is cyclical, and looked at the four stages it goes through during each cycle. All very interesting, but how can we use this to invest more success-fully?

Let's start with an implication that sounds mundane but is actually very important: property is cyclical, therefore prices surging and falling back are nothing to be overly concerned about. If you only listen to what the media says, the message is always "everything's great!" or "everything's terrible!" – and it can seem totally random as to which is the case at any given time. It's reassuring to know that it's not random at all, and it's driven by fundamental economic principles.

The next implication is that if the cycle moves predictably through its four stages, you can see what's coming next. Fred Harrison claims evidence going back hundreds of years for the cycle's duration averaging 18 years, but I prefer not to dwell on that – because it invites argument about whether the "18 year" claim is true, and distracts from the central message. Even if you don't know precisely *when* something is coming, knowing that it *will* come makes a big difference. For example, you're less likely to panic and sell at the bottom of the market if you know that prices *won't* fall forever – they will inevitably recover.

Not only that, but you can gauge where we are now (and there-fore what's coming next) by looking at signals out there in the world. For example, are you seeing more and more cranes as you walk around town, and prices seem to be taking a bit of a dip after a few years of slow and steady growth? Then you could surmise that we're well into the recovery phase, and you can strap yourself in the explosive phase yet to come.

We've also seen that the "smart money" and the amateur in-vestor behave differently from each other throughout the cycle.

For example, just as casual investors are lining up a huge mortgage to grab their piece of the boom, those in the know are quietly selling their stock and stockpiling cash for the crash to come. In other words, most people buy high and sell low – exactly the opposite of what they should be doing.

I can't promise that knowing about the cycle will give you the degree of knowledge and mental toughness you need to buy at rock bottom and sell at the very height of the market. And nor do you need to – remember, each cycle starts at a higher level than the previous one, so "buy and hold for 20 years" is still a perfectly valid strategy. What's more, if you sit around for years waiting for prices to fall, you're missing out on a lot of income.

There are, though, four very basic "rules" you should follow as an investor – and now you know about the cycle, it should be easier for you to do so:

1. Don't panic and sell a property just because prices are falling. Thanks to the cycle, you know that prices *won't* go to zero and it won't be that long (in the great scheme of things) until they're back beyond where they were.

2. Don't put yourself in a position where you're *forced* to sell at the wrong point in the cycle. This is the most important point of all, and I'm dedicating an entire chapter to it next.

3. Don't get carried away (like everyone else is) during the winner's curse phase. This is the worst possible time to

buy a property, because prices will soon fall and won't recover to the level you bought at until relatively late in the next cycle. It's an even *worse* time to remortgage and use the cash for fancy cars and holidays. You might think you'd never be so daft, but plenty of people were last time around.

4. Don't get mislead by the media. As we've already seen, the messages they pump out around the key turning points of the cycle are almost exactly the opposite of what professional investors are doing. Putting on the blinkers and shutting it all out is easier said than done, but it's vital for making the right decision.

Just stick to those basics and you'll already be doing a heck of a lot better than most amateur investors. But if you want to push it even further, there are some more advanced options that knowledge of the cycle makes possible:

1. Be a seller when everyone else is buying. The winner's curse phase is a terrible time to buy, but a *great* time to sell. You don't have to sell everything, but it's the perfect opportunity to offload any properties that haven't performed as well as you'd hoped – and get someone to pay silly money to take it off your hands. Alternatively, you *could* sell everything. The idea is anathema to most small private investors, but it's what the big institutional investors do: set an exit price at the point of purchase, sell once you've made the anticipated gains, and re-buy in a

location that's at a different point in the cycle (and therefore has greater growth potential). Speaking of which…

2. Be a buyer when everyone else is selling. It doesn't even have to be at rock bottom: people's memories of a crash last longer than the economic reality, so the estate agents' offices remain empty well after prices have stabilised and started to creep upwards again.

3. *Prepare* to be a buyer when everyone else is selling, by boosting your cash in the bank during the winner's curse phase. Mortgage lending will immediately tighten when prices take a tumble, so even if you're brave enough to buy you might not be able to access the funds. Instead, you can raise funds in advance by selling poorly performing properties or refinancing (to sensible levels) properties you've already got. Hang on, didn't I just say that remortgaging in the winner's curse phase was a terrible idea? No, only if you're using the equity you release to buy overpriced properties or fund your lifestyle. If you put the cash in the bank, you can use it later to buy properties at a discount – or just repay the money if you change your mind.

So, I hope by now you're a believer in the wonders of the property cycle. You don't have to scrap "buy and hold" and start timing the market instead – although you can if you want to. Even if you just stick to the very basics, you'll do very nicely indeed.

As I said, the most fundamental lesson of all is to be aware that it's an inevitability that a crash *will* happen at some point. That's why I've dedicated the next chapter to making sure you're able to survive it – because after all, there's no point in going to all the trouble of building up a property portfolio just to lose it when the economy takes a turn for the worse.

Chapter 17

Surviving a property crash

Most people are terrified of falling house prices – but as we now know from the property cycle, it's inevitable that prices will slump at certain points. If you're holding for the long term, it doesn't matter all that much – as long as you're able to hang on until they pick up again.

Preparing for a crash, then, involves putting your portfolio into a position where you won't be forced to sell, and can calmly ride things out until the inevitable recovery arrives. Let's look at how to do just that.

Why do investors go bust?

To know how to structure your portfolio to survive a crash, it helps to understand the sequence of events that leads to a property investor "going under":

1. The portfolio is in a "negative cashflow" situation, meaning that rents don't cover expenses and the investor must subsidise the portfolio with cash from elsewhere. This could result from a spike in interest rates – which didn't

happen with the 2008 crash, but often does. Alternatively the investor may have been in negative cashflow even at low interest rates, because they were speculating on capital growth rather than keeping an eye on income.

2.   At some point, the investor can't put in any more cash, and therefore can't afford to meet the portfolio's expenses. In order to avoid repossession, they're forced to sell quickly at a low price – low because prices will be falling anyway, and even lower because of the need to sell fast.

3.   If the sale price is greater than the mortgage balance, the investor has "survived" the recession but is left with a smaller portfolio and less equity than they had previously. But if they were highly leveraged and they can't sell at a high enough price to cover the mortgage, that means repossession and possibly bankruptcy.

The key then is to avoid progressing beyond the first point by making sure the portfolio is never losing money. As long as it's at least breaking even, you can hold on for as long as you need to – allowing time for prices to increase again. Yes, the bank could call in your mortgage or request extra collateral if the loan-to-value is now higher than it was originally, but in reality they're unlikely to force a repossession at a time when everything is falling apart. Repossessing a property actually costs them a lot of money, so they'd rather have the income from the repayments than be left having to take it over and dispose of it when prices are low anyway.

A recession-proof portfolio

There are two ways to survive a recession. One is the risk-free option of buying properties only in cash, so repossession isn't an option and you survive by default. If you can do that and still reach your financial goals, that's great – but most of us will want to use leverage to boost our returns.

The other option is to use your knowledge of the property cycle to make sure you're taking on the *right* level of risk at the *right* time. Clearly, this is the option I prefer – and in this section, I'll show you what that looks like. The only prerequisite is that you believe that the property cycle exists (not necessarily the length of the cycle – just that it's cyclical at all) and that you have a basic ability to look around and form a somewhat accurate opinion about what's going on around you.

Hold property that yields well

A portfolio that yields well will keep you out of trouble by giving you plenty of "headroom" for expenses to increase while you still remain profitable. This is where the notion of "stress testing" your portfolio comes in: with other expenses held constant, at what interest rate would you stop making money and start breaking even?

There's no right answer to what "break even" interest rate is acceptable. Interest rates have historically been as high as 15%, and that could happen again. However, I consider that exceptionally unlikely, and it's even more unlikely that they would *stay* that high for more than a few months – meaning that my cash reserve would only need to make up the difference for a short period of time.

There's no right answer, but there is a wrong answer: "no margin for error at all". Mortgage rates are currently more or less as low as they can possibly be: banks can access money for next to nothing, and there's a certain minimum margin they need on top to cover their costs and make a profit. If you're buying a property that only just breaks even now, it can only get worse – so really, gambling on capital growth is the only benefit of owning it.

As we learned earlier though, lenders are required to "stress test" most forms of borrowing at an interest rate of 5.5%, so in practice it's difficult to make a purchase that doesn't have some headroom baked in.

Maintain cash reserves

A loss-making portfolio caused by a spike in interest rates isn't a disaster as long as you've got enough supplementary cash to throw in to meet mortgage payments. You should have cash reserves anyway to cover void periods and unexpected maintenance expenses, so it's just a case of making sure the fund is large enough to see you through.

How big should the reserve fund be? Disappointingly, I don't have a satisfying answer to this – although of course, the more highly leveraged you are the more cash you might need to put in if interest rates increase. One investor I know argues for having 20% of total borrowings in available cash at any one time. I understand his logic, but I can't bear to see so much cash sitting around losing money in real terms after factoring in inflation.

Conversely, I know another investor who holds back very little because he claims he could move all his personal spending to a 0% credit card if needs be, and cover the portfolio with what he normally spends on himself. I take the middle path and just keep a reassuring lump of money in my current account, which is sufficiently large to be comforting while not giving me anxiety at the opportunity cost of not having it invested elsewhere.

If your portfolio is only moderately geared, you could always boost your cash reserves by remortgaging to release equity. I'm about to warn against expanding at the wrong time, but taking on debt to hold cash in reserve is an exception: in a crisis, an extra £20,000 in the bank will do you a lot more good than having monthly expenses that are £100 lower.

Don't expand at the wrong time

As you'll remember from our discussion of the property cycle, the (roughly) two years leading up to the peak and the crash are known as the "winner's curse" – because bidding is out of control, and whoever "wins" ends up holding a hopelessly overpriced property and will struggle when values fall.

Even if the only thing you take away from this chapter is to avoid over-extending yourself during this period, you'll have removed a massive portion of the risk that property investment entails.

That's easier said than done, because banks will be throwing money at you and the value of your portfolio will have increased – and in a way that makes it a good time to take on new debt on good terms. The problem is that anything you can buy with that debt will be worth substantially less in a couple of years' time.

So don't remortgage to buy overpriced property, and certainly don't remortgage to upgrade your lifestyle because you think you're rich now. What you *can* do is to strategically remortgage to put more cash in the bank if the circumstances are right – because as I've said, in the event of a crash you'll be better off with a lump of cash in the bank than slightly lower monthly outgoings.

Distribute equity unevenly

You can also strategically remortgage to redistribute equity throughout your portfolio. If you have two properties of similar value, you're better off having one mortgaged to 75% and the other to 25% than you are having both mortgaged to 50%.

Why? Because if you're forced to sell a property to raise cash to cover your other outgoings, you only want to sell *one* property. If you've got just a little equity in several properties and prices fall, you might need to sell *all* of them to meet your obligations.

This point is a little more advanced and probably won't be necessary if you've been sufficiently cautious in other respects, but it's another tool to use if you want to make sure your portfolio is totally bulletproof.

Chapter 18

Exits

So far in Part 3 we've talked about financing the growth of your portfolio, nurturing it through the property cycle and making sure it stays intact in the event of a crash. All being well, you'll approach the Werther's Originals phase of your life as the owner of a collection of properties that have given you great financial success – but then what?

Given the title of this book, it's only appropriate that we conclude by giving some attention to exit strategies – by which I mean exiting the stage of being an active investor and turning your thoughts towards retirement. I'm going to assume that you've been buying properties with interest-only mortgages, because if you own your properties outright there's really nothing to think about – you can just hold everything for the income until you shuffle off, then pass them on to a lucky relative/cattery. When there are mortgage balances involved though, the matter requires a bit more thought.

There will be tax consequences for each approach too, but I won't get into this in detail: it depends far too much on your personal circumstances and how you've structured your portfolio for me to say anything useful. And in any case, the rules might all have changed by the time you get to this point in your life. I'll just remind you to get professional advice at the appropriate time before taking any drastic action, and leave it at that.

So, what are your options?

Hold forever

There's a popular misconception that you can't get mortgages beyond the age of 60ish. This is true for residential mortgages because the assumption is that you need to be earning a wage to pay it off each month, but isn't the case for buy-to-let. You can take out loans that don't need to be repaid until you're more than 100 years old – which means you could conceivably just keep on going until you drop, with no need to exit at all.

(Your heirs would then be left scrambling to refinance or sell the properties to pay the inheritance tax bill, but it's for you to decide how much you like your heirs and how bothered you'll be about their inconvenience once you're dead.)

The risk to this approach is circumstances changing once you're already retired and relying on the income that your properties produce. I don't personally want concerns about interest rates to put me off my bingo game, but for some people this strategy will be a totally valid option.

Sell half

OK, not necessarily half, but a common exit strategy is to sell enough properties to pay off the debt on the rest – so that you hold your remaining portfolio free and clear. Then, as long as you've made appropriate allowances for expenses, you've got a pretty much bulletproof source of income in retirement. Whatever happens to capital values isn't of any concern (because you're never going to sell them), and your income should theoretically be inflation-proof because rents tend to rise in line with incomes (and incomes rise with inflation over the long term).

The thing to remember is that for all the years you've held your properties, their value should have increased while your debt remains static. If you haven't been refinancing too aggressively, what was originally a 75% loan-to-value portfolio could have fallen to well below 50% by the time you're ready to retire. You might even find that you could sell just one property to clear the balances on the rest.

There's capital gains tax to factor in if your properties have made strong gains over a large number of years, but that doesn't mean there's necessarily anything wrong with this strategy. It's just something to take into account, and to attempt to minimise by selling gradually over a number of years and making use of personal allowances.

The only real cause for concern with this strategy is that you might end up without appropriate diversification after selling whatever is necessary to shift the mortgage balances. Being left with just one or two properties that cover your expenses is nice and simple from a management point of view, but also risky: non-paying tenants in one of your properties would cut your "pension" in half until the situation is resolved.

Liquidate

It could be that in your old age, you want nothing to do with property at all. In that case, there's nothing to stop you from selling the lot and investing the proceeds in another asset class. No, it's not particularly tax-efficient because of capital gains tax, but there's more to life than paying as little tax as possible.

In terms of diversification, this isn't a terrible idea. If you could make roughly the same net return from a couple of unencumbered properties or a globally diversified portfolio of stocks and bonds, the latter might give you better peace of mind.

Restructure

The options above are all totally valid strategies, but the best option of all is likely to be a mix-and-match of all of them, depending on your risk tolerance and income requirements. For example, you could:

- Sell a couple of properties to raise cash to put into stocks and bonds for diversification.

- Sell another to reduce your loan-to-value.

- Keep the rest for income, with very low mortgages so you're not overly worried about changes to interest rates.

If you're relying on income from your portfolio in retirement, there's a strong argument for restructuring in some way. The game has changed: your focus may previously have been on capital growth, but now what matters is rock-solid income. You might be holding properties that don't yield particularly well, or even properties that you bought just because there was an opportunity to do a refurb and recycle your funds. Maybe you even want to offload your leasehold properties in favour of freehold, so you don't have the uncertainty of service charges and dwindling leases to worry about.

This is why the advice to "buy and hold forever" makes sense in some respects, but is incomplete: if a property was bought for a particular purpose and it's no longer doing that job, selling might make sense. As investors, we shouldn't be emotionally attached to any property.

CONCLUSION

If I had to guess, I'd say that having read this book, you won't do anything with it. You won't end up investing in property, and your life will look much the same in a few years as it does now.

It's nothing personal – it's just that statistically speaking, most people won't. As great as the rewards of property investment sound, it's just too risky/intimidating/time-consuming for most people to bother with. Far safer to just keep going to work and doing what everyone else does, even if you know deep down that the outcome won't be as good.

In this book, I've done everything I can to boost your chances of taking action. I've started out by showing you what results are possible – even if you're not the greatest investor in the world, and even if you've got limited time and resources to dedicate to it. I've taken you step by step through the process so you know what to expect and can see that every obstacle can be overcome, and I've given you a vision for going beyond that first property to create something really meaningful.

If you do pull it off, you'll have done something truly rare. Many people have no real assets to speak of. Most people own nothing more than their own house and maybe a small private pension. Only a tiny percentage of the UK population owns more than one investment property. Some people picking up this book will be in a position to achieve this goal easily and others will have to work very hard – but in every case, it *can* be done and it's well worth doing.

Let me leave you with what I think are the two most important ideas in property investment – even though I almost never see them discussed.

The first is something I've touched on several times in this book: the triangle of capital, timeframe and effort. The less you have of one, the more you'll need to lean on the others.

If you're working 60 hours per week, have £20,000 in savings and want to have a monthly income of £5,000 from property by this time next year, can you do it? Almost certainly not, because you're low on all three key elements. What if you start with a million pounds in the bank? Then you probably can. Ditto if you extend the timeframe to ten years, or quit your job to work 100-hour weeks in property to make it happen, or some combination of the three.

I consider this to be the absolute key to having realistic expecta-tions about what you can achieve. And realistic expectations are important because otherwise you run the risk of getting discour-aged and quitting early, or embarking on harebrained schemes that involve taking on too much risk.

The second key idea is that for most of us, property investment is only part of the picture when it comes to creating a better life for ourselves (whatever we take that to mean).

This isn't true for everyone. Some people will be naturally gifted dealmakers, or work preternaturally hard, or conduct projects with such flair and imagination that they're immensely profitable – and they'll make an excellent living from property as a result.

For most of us though, property will only *truly* work for us as part of a general program of personal development. It involves having your personal finances in order so you've got funds to invest and are creditworthy. It involves being able to set realistic and meaningful goals, and making steady progress towards them despite the inevitable setbacks. It involves knowing yourself, so you can set a strategy that matches your skills and attitudes. It involves the flexibility to change tack when circumstances change. And it probably involves being a bit weird – having an individualistic streak that allows you to ignore what everyone else is doing, and having enough self-control to place your long-term interests ahead of immediate gratification to an unusual degree.

Consequently, being a successful property investor comes down to far more than making the right decision about whether to buy House A or Flat B. It's about transforming yourself into a successful person *in general*, with property being just part of that equation. If that sounds a bit woo-woo or over-intellectualised… well, maybe it is. But I rarely encounter a successful investor who isn't an impressive person more generally, and I don't think that's any kind of coincidence.

So there's your challenge: be one of the few who takes action, work through everything we've covered in this book from start to finish, and end up financially comfortable as a result. I hope I've made it sound sufficiently difficult, because it is. But it's a whole lot of fun too.

NOW KEEP ON LEARNING!

Now you've read this book, you're better prepared than most to start investing – but there's still plenty to learn, and things are changing all the time.

To keep up with all the latest changes and other important property and economic news, I recommend you do these three things:

1. Register your purchase of this book at **propertygeek.net/extra**. This will give you access to some extra materials, and you'll start receiving my Sunday newsletter – where I share the top property news stories of the week, with a bit of commentary about what they mean for you.

2. Subscribe to The Property Podcast at **propertyhub.net/podcast**, where there's a new episode every Thursday morning.

3. Check out the wealth of educational material we're constantly adding to at Property Hub (**propertyhub.net**) – including

videos, free courses, and the forum where you can join in the discussion with thousands of other investors.